Messy

The guide to living lighter

and giving less forks

KATIE DEAN

Copyright © 2019 Katie Dean

First published by the kind press, 2019

All rights reserved. No part of this book may be reproduced, stored in a retrieval system or transmitted in any form or by any means, electronic, mechanical photocopying, recording, or otherwise, without written permission from the author and publisher.

The author of this book does not dispense medical advice or prescribe the use of any technique as a form of treatment for physical, emotional, or medical problems without the advice of a physician, either directly or indirectly. The intent of the author is only to offer information of a general nature to help you in your quest for wellbeing. While the publisher and author have used their best efforts in preparing this book, the material in this book is of the nature of general comment only. In the event you use any of the information in this book for yourself, the author and the publisher assume no responsibility for your actions.

Cover design by Elle Lynn

Cover concept by Sarah Baume

Interior design by Ida Jansson

Cataloguing-in-Publication entry is available from the National Library Australia.

ISBN 978-0-6485917-1-9 (Paperback)

ISBN 978-0-6485917-3-3 (Ebook)

Printed in Australia, UK, and USA

This one's for us.

We were never really lost, sweet peas,

our confidence was merely waiting to be found.

The first bit

Ever heard the saying, "What screws us up most in life is the picture in our head of how it's meant to be."

    I *get* that.

Life is full of contradictions, lessons and laughter, calm amongst chaos, more questions than answers, but the biggest game changer was realising this life *thing* we're doing was always going to be **Messy.** We all get challenged. That's the point. I have spent my life gathering evidence to support ways to live lightly; how to find certainty within oneself, and how to give way less shits about what's not important.

Once I stopped waiting for things to be easy, I unlocked a whole new *ease* to life I never knew was there. There's no such thing as bad weather, just poor clothing choices, so let's double down, get set for all conditions and embrace the ultra-feely mess this human-ing gig is.

    Are you ready to see things a little differently, sweet potato?

    Thought so. I like you already.

    Onwards, friend.

Get your contents here!

The first bit	*5*
Introduction: It's a bit of a mess	*11*
1. LOWER THE BAR. NO LOWER. A LITTLE LOWER. THERE YOU GO	18
2. WAITING FOR THINGS TO BE EASY, IS ACTUALLY MAKING THEM HARD	24
3. YOU CAN'T FIX SOMETHING THAT'S NOT BROKEN	31
4. C L O S U R E	36
5. SCARED ACTUALLY	38
6. DO MORE BY DOING LESS	44
7. THE STRENGTH IS IN THE SOFTENING	50
8. IT'S NOT ME, IT'S YOU	55
9. YOU'RE NOT WHO YOU WERE	61
10. MAYBE THE BEST WAY FORWARD IS TO STOP	67
11. LEVEL UP	72
12. FAILURE IS A FEELING, NOT A DESTINATION	76
13. IT'S GOING TO FEEL WORSE, BEFORE IT FEELS BETTER	81
14. STOP LOOKING FOR THINGS TO FIX AND YOU'LL FIX EVERYTHING	88

15. YEAH, NAH	93
16. IT'S NOT YOU, IT'S ME	98
17. THE FIRST YEAR AFTER THE ONE BEFORE IS THE HARDEST	103
18. TRUST YOUR GUT	109
19. I'M NOT HERE TO PLEASE ANYONE, THANK YOU	115
20. BLAME. WHEN YOU BREAK YOUR OWN HEART	121
21. REMOVE THE WORD 'JUST'. IT'S LAME	127
22. EVOLVE OR REPEAT	132
23. FACT OR FEELING	139
24. INSIDE OUTSIDE, OUTSIDE INSIDE	143
25. GETTING ANXIOUS ABOUT GETTING ANXIOUS	148
26. YOUR MESS WILL BE YOUR MAKING	152
27. DON'T WORRY	156
28. IT'S THE TITS	161
29. DO NO HARM, BUT TAKE NO SHIT	166
30. STOP SAYING YES TO SHIT YOU HATE	170
31. 'NO' IS A COMPLETE SENTENCE	174
32. HOLD YOUR GAZE	179
33. YOU'RE HEARING, BUT ARE YOU LISTENING?	184
34. YOU COMPLETE ME	187
35. SHOULD-ING ALL OVER YOURSELF	192
36. SILENCE IS THE BEST SOUND	197
37. HURT PEOPLE, HURT PEOPLE	202
38. WHO DOES SHE THINK SHE IS?	206
39. ALL'S FAIR IN LOVE AND WAR	210
40. SOMETIMES SAYING NOTHING, SAYS THE MOST	217
41. BOUNDARIES ARE NOT FENCES	221
42. INTROVERTED EXTROVERT	230

43. SAY 'YES' TO THE DRESS	236
44. DO YOU LIKE WHAT YOU SEE?	242
45. I WILL WHEN I HAVE	247
46. LAUGH IT OFF	252
47. I AM WILLING	257
48. IT'S NOT YOUR JOB TO BE EASY	262
49. JUST BECAUSE THEY BELIEVE IT, DOESN'T MAKE IT TRUE	266
50. GETTING BIKINI BODY READY	270
51. THE GOOD GIRL MUST DIE	275
52. A WOMAN'S WORTH	285
53. ALL EYES ARE ON YOU	287
54. HIGH HOPES	292
The last bit	*295*
About the author	*297*
Resources	*298*
Messy Contributors	300
Acknowledgements	302
Glossary of Anti-Self-Help-y terminology	*304*

*Not because I have to,
but because I get to.*

Introduction:

IT'S A BIT OF A MESS

I want to start by saying that within my life I have used the words 'shit show' more often than I thought, but it's probably not for the reasons you'd think.

If we were to put my life on paper, no doubt it would look a little, to get all technical here, PWFFFOOOOOR, YIKES! But it's not the big benchmarks that do it. It's the smaller, less headline-grabbing moments that undo me. It's the mad rush to get the kids to pre-school. It's the random poo the baby did on the rug and stood in. It's the in and out of the car, the packing to get somewhere, the attempting to go to the bathroom in peace, or getting the washing on the line before the mouldy smell arrives and you end up washing the entire load again, again. These are the unavoidable and messy parts of life we all have. The coffee spills on a white shirt. The moments thinking, *what in the fork did they mean by that?* The saga of, *will they, won't they call?*

It's a bit of a mess.

Messy, messy, messy.

These are the little moments we all have. It's just whether we choose to get stuck in them. We're all doubting our ability to do what we set out to do. We're all thinking someone can probably do this better. We're sure we're doing something *wrong* but we're not so sure how to fix it.

I want us all to stop.

Stop trying so hard.

Stop pushing so much.

To understand the *messy* is where the magic is.

My name is Katie, and welcome to *Messy*.

I really flipped my life on its head when, at sixteen weeks pregnant with my second son, I took a sledgehammer to the 'picture-perfect' life I was living, asked for a separation and became a 'Solo Mum'.

While so much that unravelled after my decision was heartbreaking, stomach churning and all the things you could imagine, I never once doubted myself and the decision I ultimately had to make. I'll never go into the reasons that led to what bought it all to a head that night because that's not what's important. However, I put myself on the path of peace, but not before I came at it like a wrecking ball. Both me and Miley Cyrus.

On average in Australia, one in three women experience anxiety, almost 90% of Australians experience disordered sleeping, and a third will experience full-blown insomnia. It's safe to say we have a lot going on upstairs, but I know we can do a lot to calm our farms. The sooner we stop trying to micromanage every possible outcome and every possible situation, the sooner we open up the possibility of *calm*. It's easy to think by having a solution figured out for all the things *waaaay* in advance, *that* would be the key to finding our calm.

Yeah, nah!

That's not how this shizzle works. The more we try to control everything, predict and foresee everything, the more likely we are to miss out on the gifts. So, how on earth do we—especially A-type, ambitious, driven, project-based types—let go of the need to control and lean into the unknown, with peace and love?

That's what this book is about.

In the next fifty-four chapters, we will shine a light on the outdated thinking holding us back and unlearn some dialogue that wasn't really ours to begin with.

By the end of this book, I hope you feel grounded in your potential, brave enough to go after what you want. And to learn a lot about yourself and your enough-ness along the way. Life isn't meant to be flawless. It's not meant to be delicate and life is rarely picture-perfect. It's messy, it's contradictory, and it's in the seemingly mundane moments, if you're willing to let them in, magic truly unfolds.

I got a message from a beautiful friend last night; she was worrying about how difficult she was finding an *exceptionally* hard situation and was looking for some ways to fix the situation. My answer: Let it be difficult. It's meant to be. My words, 'What you are going through right now is forking hard, and the only way it will get easier is to keep going.'

Negative feelings don't need fixing. They are there for a reason.

Sometimes life is *actually* hard.

Sometimes situations are really gut-wrenchingly difficult.

Sometimes our hearts will actually break.

If you lose someone you love, it's completely normal to feel devastated, depressed and lost. Those feelings are there because you loved someone and now they won't be there as you remembered them. That will never be easy. Trying to skim over the feelings won't bring them back. In actual fact, it will bypass so much of the healing process for you.

You dodge the hurt; you miss the healing.

If you have your heart stomped on by someone who used to look really great, that will *not* feel like a good time. You will go through a huge array of emotions and each of them is signifying a different level of understanding, processing and healing. There is absolutely nothing wrong with you for not enjoying a breakup. Breakups are rough. It's okay to feel sad, shitty and about seventeen other feelings alike. That's an entirely normal internal response to a shattering external situation. A heavy heart will lighten when it's meant to and not before we've learnt what is there for us to learn about ourselves.

Depression largely comes from suppressing your feelings for too long. If you have avoided or been scared to face your feelings and your truth, then you will naturally find yourself in the shadows. A place where hope feels far-off, numb is an everyday occurrence and you are down so low you can no longer feel the warmth of the sun. Before you proclaim or tell yourself you are broken or less than, please look at what you have faced and what you are moving through.

> **Do you feel you should handle things better?**
> **What is actually going on around you, now?**
> **Is there an explanation why this may be a challenging time?**

I bet you, I mean, I seriously would give you everything in my wallet you are not broken. In fact, you are forking brave and resilient AF— because you've probably faced something, or a series of things that have totally rocked you. If that's the case, you aren't broken, babe. You're a badass Queen who deserves a medal because putting one foot in front of the other when you feel like falling apart is the most together thing you can do.

Nothing goes away until we learn what we need to learn.

Nothing leaves us alone until we acknowledge what we need to acknowledge.

And nothing has the power to make us more uncomfortable than our very own feelings about how we believe we should be feeling. #Savage. So, I urge you, sweet friend (It's not too forward of me to say that now, is it? I mean I think I've sworn at you twice already so that pretty much means we're friends now. #amiright?), before you think there's something wrong with you. I want you to look and see what you're dealing with.

If you find yourself in a shit storm, you won't be smelling great. How long this stands to affect you comes down to how you choose to handle it. If you refuse to acknowledge what's going on and deny you're even in said poo storm, you will carry that crap with you for a really long time. However, if you acknowledge you're in hectic weather, up to your eyeballs in shit, then you're more likely to do what is needed to rid yourself of the stench and come out shiny and new. Not all storms are meant to scare us you know, some storms are there to wash us clean.

Now, before we go any further, can we all just take a moment to be glad that shit doesn't actually fall from the sky.

    Namaste.

Putting one foot in front of the other when you feel like falling apart is

the most together thing you can do.

1.
LOWER THE BAR. NO LOWER. A LITTLE LOWER. THERE YOU GO

I'll say it straight-up. True happiness lies within lowering your standards.

I know, I know, you probably just took a huge breath. Or maybe you held it or thought *this bitch is off her meds*. Now, friend, that is a little offensive but I'm really not one to take things personally anymore. Plus, I get it. Society has always taught us to aim high, to be the best version of ourselves and try for the very best things in life, right?

Right.

That's still 100% a beautiful way to be.

I'm not suggesting for a second we lower our goals, look for less in a partner. This idea of lowering the bar isn't about not hoping for the best, it's about judging ourselves less.

When I had my first son, I used to hold myself to such a high standard of perfection it was forking crippling at times. For instance, I had a set way in my mind of all the jobs that needed to get done before I'd leave the house in the morning. In reality, this started long before I even became a mum. I held such a tight grip on everything I'd unconsciously created these impossible thorough daily tasks. I thought if I loosened the reins, my entire world would unravel. The to-dos were the key to my happiness and ability to feel content. The main area where I've let go of the micromanaging is my home. *Ha!* That makes me giggle as I write this because it sounds so bloody awful. While we're not living in a crap shack, life is a fair bit messier. It's a little softer around the edges. The priorities have shifted and getting out the door is far more important than what I have to step over or let go of to get us there.

I choose how we roll.

Not the other way around.

There're a few more toys around, we often leave the dishes until morning and the kids ride their bikes inside because it makes them happy.

I chose the thug life; it didn't choose me.

Or is that meant to be the other way around? I'm not really sure but let's get back to my beautifully lowered expectations. Perhaps my time as a stewardess onboard superyachts where nothing could be out of place led to my overachieving desire to have a home that looked like we didn't actually live in it. On the yachts, the crew and I would communicate with each other all day via a radio attached to our hips. As soon as the guests would leave a room we would sweep in and rearrange the cushions and room, so it looked like *they* were never there. It was a surreal experience and gave me the 'stew eye'. This is like a domestic superpower.

Stew eye: ability to judge a small room from top to bottom with one sweeping glance and decide what needs to get altered to bring a room back to square. That's yachty talk for neat AF—!

For me, once I had two beautiful babies, I struggled to get all the things done I'd need to before I left the house or even give myself permission to sit down. Things like clearing breakfast, cleaning the dishes on the sink, tidying the messy lounge room. They were all huge no-no's.

> **Is there an area of your life that holds a lot of stress in how you deal with it?**
>
> **How can you lower your standards—in a good way—in a way that releases you, empowers you and increases your happiness, presence and sense of identity?**
>
> **How can you reset your bar so the aching, unachievable expectations you set are no longer so impossible to reach, and so disappointing when you fall short of them?**

Keeping my home this way was redic.

I was always late.

I was always stressed.

And that energy would always rub off on my two boys. I constantly felt like I was failing because if you've ever been around children—I know you have—then you know they love a mess. They're all about it. It makes them happy and they don't give a flying f— about time.

I was on the phone to my friend, Jess, telling her how hard it was to get out the house, even to clean up breakfast before leaving for the morning. She laughed at me. Jess said that with each new child, you need to lower the bar a little. Jess is a kick-ass Mumma of four, who also knits a large majority of her children's clothes and cooks most things from scratch.

I am not like Jess.

At first, if truth be told, I thought Jess had lost her mind. *Leave the dishes? Lower the bar? What on earth is she thinking?* Then I realised Jess was onto something. If I wanted to make it through the rest of my thirties with any hair left, then I should probs give this lower bar thing a go.

So, I did.

The first time felt like I was cheating on myself. Then, when I began to see the rewards, I was hooked. This was actually the best. I lowered my expectations of what I could achieve in the home within a day and raised the amount of quality time I had with my kids and decreased all our stress levels. I mean, who knew that letting the dishes pile up could hold such empowered freedom. I now only clean up the toys once at the end of the day. I will clear a path occasionally, but I also like to live on the edge. It can be a bit of a game of Russian Roulette when you're carrying the washing and can't see your feet which always keeps things spicy. *Will I make it out today? Am I going to step on Lego? Will we finally find that missing piece of the puzzle we've been looking for?*

You know, it's really beautiful if you let it be.

It wasn't about turning into a sloth and letting us live like pigs, because I assure you we don't, mostly. It was about taking the time to re-examine the rules we were living by and seeing if they were, in fact, really true for us. I'm totally down for a little mess in the kitchen if it means we get out the door with only mild whisper-screaming. I'm all in for a spontaneous dance party if it means I don't have to empty the dishwasher. I'm not sure why I eye roll myself into another dimension every time I have to empty the darn thing because it makes our life easier.

It's never too late to examine your own rules and create a new set that feel good for you and help you live life better. For you, lowering your standard might not be about household cleanliness. It could be the way you dress. Why not buy five of the same t-shirts and rotate them instead of wasting time and energy co-ordinating outfits in the morning? It could be the amount you socialise, or how tidy or untidy your car is. It could mean saying no to more work opportunities because you admit you just don't have the capacity to work at the same pace you once did, for now anyway. It's the expectation you place on yourself or others that is strangling your enjoyment from every interaction. A conscious choice to see your success and happiness differently is a fabulous place to start to chill out.

Lowering the bar doesn't mean lowering your standards. It means allowing yourself to be happy with less and being content more. There's really no reason why you can't choose to be happy right now. Don't you think it's time you enjoyed the journey?

    Yeah, me too.

Be open to being

happier with less.

2.
WAITING FOR THINGS TO BE EASY, IS ACTUALLY MAKING THEM HARD

Have you ever judged yourself for struggling?

Spoiler alert: I totally have. If you have ever struggled and felt bad for struggling or guilty because you 'shouldn't' be struggling, then bring it in, sister, I want to give you a hug.

I want you to take a second and bring to mind the last time you felt like you were failing at this life gig. I would give you my last two chewy mints and a bliss ball to bet if you paused for a second, you'd see something profound. You'd see the elements of your life have conspired together to present you with a situation, or a time in your life that quite frankly was forking hard.

I have had three separate conversations this week with smart, strong and incredibly capable women feeling a little beaten around the edges by life. These women were understandably stressed, strung out or questioning all the things. I could hear it and see the concerned expression on their faces. It broke my heart because I've been there; I get that feeling of overwhelm and failure. I've felt that vibe that there's something *wrong* with us for feeling this way. Maybe if *we* changed, scheduled more, did something different, that would mean things would be easier. There always seems to be this idea *we* must be doing something wrong for things to feel anything other than joyful, rosy or filled to the eyeballs with gratitude.

Yeah, that feels familiar and I am putting my foot down.

My answer is NO. Just NO.

No, you are not failing.

No, you are not 'hopeless', 'broken', 'incapable'.

In reality, when you feel you're drowning, it's more than likely you *are* in fact having a completely normal response to the phase or situation you're in right now. Some phases and situations are just hard. It's that whole cause vs effect thing.

There have been countless times where I have felt as though I'm drowning in motherhood. Where I couldn't find a way to come up for air amidst the growing weight of tantrums, daily life with a newborn, endless piles of laundry and self-doubt. I never had time to ferment my own sauerkraut and I didn't always get to the farmers markets. Many times the kids had rice crackers and yoghurt pouches for a meal because everything else would end up on the floor.

I judged myself so harshly. I said the most hectic things to and about myself.

Everyone else can do this better than you.

Maybe you weren't meant to be a mother.

You're failing. No one said it would be like this.

Gnarly, gnarly! Really depressing self-talk.

> **Where in your life are you judging yourself?**
> **Where in your life do you believe you should be doing better?**

Here's the thing, when I just googled the words 'I feel like I'm failing'. 1, 330,000,000 results came up. That is a ginormous figure, a perfect example that many of us feel we should be doing better in life, at some point. We are no strangers to feeling less than and are far too harsh on ourselves for simply being human. If you have been judging yourself, you are in incredible company.

If you find yourself in a shit storm, inevitably you won't smell great. Likewise if you lose your job, have your heart broken, or have to grieve the loss of a loved one, you are absolutely 100% going to feel bloody awful—for a time. If you have children and they are behaving like children, then yep, you guessed it; you will feel out of your depth, entirely overwhelmed and completely underprepared most days. Some things will stretch us. Some events or phases in life will leave us feeling broken. Surrendering might seem scary initially but I've always found it to be unbelievably comforting. The idea you're meant to be happy and smiling all the time is too much pressure and actually not attainable. Instead, how can we lean into our trickier times of life—we all have them—and not add to our worry by beating ourselves up? Allow me to change your viewpoint in three simple steps.

Embrace the ebbs

We wouldn't have the full spectrum of *emotions* if we weren't meant to feel them.

They are messengers.

They are lighthouses.

And they are part of the energy river that is passing through us.

If we stopped trying to fight them and dam them up, they could pass through us and take with them anything that's no longer meant for us.

Next time you are judging yourself for not handling things the way you believe you *should* be; I want you to look around and see if you are in fact in a challenging or hurtful or trying situation. If you see that you are, back the bus up and instead of throwing shade on yourself, congratulate yourself for surviving another day knowing that this **will** pass.

I promise you that.

It *will* in fact pass.

Accept help

You want to know something I always used to do unknowingly. Refuse help and then resent people or my life because of all the things I had to do. We aren't meant to do every single thing ourselves, yet somewhere across the line we thought we had to. Then, of course, if we didn't, we weren't batshit busy and grey around the gills we automatically failed, yeah?

This is horseshit.

First, this is the part of the conversation where if you know me, you would buckle up because I'm about to back myself with this and I may even have slides. No one comes around and gives you an award for running yourself into the ground or doing things single-handedly. If anything, you've probably isolated yourself a little more which is never the answer we're all searching for, am I right?

Second, see . . . here I go! Denying yourself the time and space to help you feel how you want to feel isn't doing anyone any favours. Saying no when your partner or family encourage you to go for a walk or out with your friends, isn't helping you or them in any way. Especially when you *really* want to go, then become shitty and resentful when *they* do something for themselves.

I've absolutely gotten all huffy about this more than once.

Don't they understand how much I have to do here?

No one will do things the way I can.

These things have to be done.

We have a routine. It must look like this.

Having fun right now doesn't fit into this super strict plan I have created for us, that helps me feel like everything is in order if we just stick to it. Honestly, am I the only one who takes any responsibility for anything around here?

Yep. Not dramatic at all. That's the space that we often get in and it's not true. Everything would be just fine, probably better than fine if we allowed ourselves to loosen the reins a little and accepted a little help, without carrying the guilt.

Feel the sunshine

Give yourself permission to enjoy your life. Give yourself the space and time to enjoy your life and fill your cup so you can give from the overflow.

> **Where in your life can you choose to see things another way?**
> **How can you choose to do that?**

It's about the little things that raise your vibe. Think, walks outside, cups of tea on the lounge, reading a book, dance-offs in the lounge room, girls' nights in. Endless possibilities. You owe it to yourself to live your life using every colour in the box, and when you've taken care of what you need, you'll draw a very different picture.

There will never be a great time to go. There will always be something that needs to get done around the house, or a project that can be tackled at work. But if you change the way you look at taking time for you and add more play, your life will grow in proportion to the amount of joy you allow yourself to have.

Examine your story. Examine what you're telling yourself about how things feel and what you *have* to do to be the woman you want to be. Do you really have to be the one who misses out all the time? Do you have to be the one who does all the things? Will your friends or kids or partner still love you if you take a little time for yourself? Yup, you will, and if you wouldn't be, then send me their names because I'mma going to get really mad and probably write them a letter.

Everything has its season and whatever one you're in, see it for what it is. Tough times don't last but resilient people do, and even resilient people can take a rest. Things don't always get easier, but we can always get smarter.

Waiting for things to get *easier,* is actually making them *harder.*

3.

YOU CAN'T FIX SOMETHING THAT'S NOT BROKEN

I can totally put my hand up and say I have 100% referred to 'uncomfortable feelings' as 'negative feelings' in my social media posts and writing. Just because something is hard, doesn't mean it needs to be avoided at all costs or that it's even negative. True story. I used to judge my feelings really heavily. If I wasn't feeling happy or joyful, I was convinced there was something wrong with me and my life. I was sure of it.

Surely everyone else is feeling jazzed all the time.

There has to be something wrong with me because I doubt myself so much.

Of course, I'm the only one on the planet who has made a fool of myself by drinking too much, saying the wrong thing and making that mistake.

I would do one of two things whenever I felt uncomfortable. I would either run from it as fast as if it were a spider in the kitchen (pretty freaken fast), which means I would avoid them at all costs (drink, work, exercise over said feelings). Or, frantically try to control, micromanage and attempt to *fix* these feelings to make them go away. Exhausting and an invitation to behold anxiety in all her glory every single time.

Look for a solution in the bottom of a chip packet to distract yourself. End up in a solid 6-hour Netflix marathon rather than face what it is your feeling. Get into a fight with someone you care about to avoid addressing the issue and end up in a way bigger shit storm because of it. The reality of all of it is that by avoiding your feels or numbing them out does nothing but delay the healing that could take place. It also extends the process dramatically and helps you develop a bunch of unhealthy coping mechanisms. Basically, it's not ideal. Uncomfortable feelings don't need fixing, they need space to move. I know that's not what you want to hear, because we all crave a quick fix, but it's true.

> **How can you support yourself during the emotions you want to rush through; sadness, regret, heartache, disappointment, loneliness, regret even?**
>
> **Instead of controlling, micromanaging and trying to do open heart surgery to cure your situation, what could you do instead that's a little more proactive than hiding under your doona?**

    If you miss someone, miss them.

If you want someone who doesn't want you back, send them love and light every time you think of them and let it be okay.

If you wished you'd have put the chocolate in the trolley at the shops, but you didn't. And now the kids are in bed and you can't go get anything sweet because you thought you were going to only eat healthy tonight, well, that's tough. You will feel that shit in your soul for a while. But don't wish this all away.

There are so many opportunities for growth in feeling all the things and also not taking yourself too seriously. When it comes to feelings and emotions, these days I'm all about not playing favourites. Not even a little. Sure, some may feel more comfortable and a lot better on you, but if you are all about enjoying the sun, then your shadow will naturally come along for the ride. It's how it works. It's the yin and the yang of your feels that makes it powerful and now I know, I mean, I freaken *know* loving your life in all conditions is where it's truly at.

If we're angry, sad or hurt, that doesn't make life any less valuable or important.

If we're confused, rejected or anxious, it doesn't make it any less of a miracle we exist. Or if we're stoked, joyful or ecstatic, it doesn't mean we've 'made it', it just means we're 'in it', just like *all* the emotions do.

This human-ing that we're doing is about feeling all the feels on the entire spectrum.

Yes, the good hair days might add a little spring to your step, but they aren't more valuable than the run-of-the-mill mum-bun-moments. When you understand each moment is as valuable as the next, it's one hell of a show this life gig, and we've got the best seats in town.

Doesn't that feel a little better already?

Yup. Thought so.

Uncomfortable

feelings

don't need fixing,

they

need space to move.

4.
CLOSURE

If you've ever craved closure on a matter and looked to someone else to give it to you, you were waiting in the wrong line, friend. I'm going to keep this short and sweet because it's really not about anyone else.

There are apologies you'll never get.

There are acknowledgments that will never be given.

There are behaviours that will never be explained.

Closure doesn't come from someone else and peace doesn't come when someone offers it to you. Peace is something you gift yourself because you'll never find happiness in the same place you lost it.

Onwards, sweet potato, onwards.

> **Where in your life can you gift yourself closure?**

Peace is something you gift yourself
because you'll never find happiness in
the same place you lost it.

5.
SCARED ACTUALLY

I can't believe it has taken me five chapters in to talk to you about my favourite topic: Fear. I've been a student of fear for the last few years—and a slave to it my entire life—it's my jam. I love it. If there was ever an emotion that could tell you bucket loads about who you are as a person, this saucy minx would be the one.

I have experienced anxiety for most of my life, but I didn't have the vocabulary or the emotional awareness to identify what I was feeling. I always felt uneasy. I feared what could go wrong and nervous about what could go right. This basically sucked the joy out of every joyful situation I encountered. I didn't understand it was safe for me to be happy, and so I lived in fear.

Fear is a chameleon.

She's super crafty like that, but once you get to know her a little, you'll realise not all fear means turn and run. Most fear means lean in and rise.

I'll say that again for you.

What if fear didn't mean turn and run and it meant lean in and rise?

I know! Revolutionary, right?

> **Where in your life do you see fear as a reason to pull back?**
>
> **What are the areas where you could now see fear as a stepping stone to rise?**

A ginormous indicator for me, that I refused to address for the longest time, was my anxiety attacks of an evening. When I was in a relationship that was no longer healthy, my anxiety would peak around bedtime. As soon as it would get dark, I'd feel myself shift into a fearful state. I'd start carrying out my mental checklist of things I needed to tick off. All I wanted to do was feel safe when I lay my head down, and I didn't want to have to worry about anything extra. I was convinced I was just overly cautious about these things. Wrong. When I ended the relationship, wouldn't you know it, once my room and my home became a relaxed and *safe* space for me again, those evening panic attacks and fear subsided.

> **Have you ever changed something in your life and the ripple effect be far more impactful than you could have imagined?**

All of our emotions are messengers. We feel what we feel as it's our body's way of communicating to us about a certain thought or story we are moving through. Very cool. Also, very confusing if you weren't raised to understand the power of your perception, and how expansive it is to understand that *you* get to decide what everything will mean for *you*.

Fear can look like a million different things.

Perfectionism.

Judgement.

Anxiety.

Overeating.

Control issues.

Stress.

Yup, stress.

When you're stressed, it's usually because you're worried about something not going to plan. You're fearful. You could be worried about having too much on your plate. Perhaps you're scared you won't be able to make it all work and you will fail. Or you could be scared shirtless you won't be able to do the thing, and everyone will judge you for it and think you're a fraud.

Fear. Fear. Fear.

Now, the buck doesn't stop here.

Once you work out what the underlying core belief is with any of your fear stories, you can work at healing them. You can meet fear with compassion, you can understand the limiting belief you hold and move through it.

WINNING!

Fear doesn't need to be met with 'punch your fear in the face' or 'live fearless' vibes. First, that's slightly psychotic. We need fear to be able to function, to make wise choices, and if you're anything like me, it's a neon sign saying 'OVER HERE! PICK ME! I'm your next opportunity for growth'. Fear's epic like that.

Most fear comes from the underlying thought; *I am not enough.*

That thought and belief is enough to give anyone a bit of a downer. I bet if you traced back some of your fears you'd see this is the seed that grew the weed. Fear of public speaking? Fear of being rejected? Fear of dancing in public? These come from a fear that you are not enough as you are.

Moving forward though, do you believe *that's* true? That you *aren't* enough? That you *aren't* worthy? Hell-to-the-No! I *know* that's not true and we've only been getting to know each other in these first five chapters, but I know it. I. Know. It.

I know any person who picks up this book—you—has a great heart. You've probably had to navigate a lot in this life so far. You really want to make sense of some of it, and you know the key to happiness is what you decide to make of this life. You want to live a life filled with all the great bits which is why you're here.

Stoked to have you here lady because you, my friend, are enough.

Track back to wherever this limiting story started and show yourself a little compassion. You are not the same person you were five years, five months or five minutes ago. You have lived; you are a badass with a great heart hell-bent on personal growth. You are resilient, and you are not going to let a story that threatens to diminish your light cast a shadow over the rest of your experiences.

You get to choose, and I know, I just know with this book in your hands and these words in your heart you will choose you.

> So now every time you feel that thought come into your mind, or you feel stressed (fear) or one of the other gateway emotions?
>
> Ask yourself the questions: What am I really feeling here?
>
> What is the story that's coming up for me?
>
> Is it true? How can I love me more in this moment?

Then you do that.

Easy-peasy lemon squeezy.

I am enough.

I have so much enough-ness.

It's crazy how much enough-ness I have.

6.

DO MORE BY DOING LESS

The word *busy* shits me to tears. Generally, not a fan at all. I think the 90s has a lot to answer for when it comes to burnout amongst women. Someone had this rad idea to make running yourself into the ground sound sexy, and attempting to juggle all the things, at once, whilst appearing to 'have it all' sound appealing.

It's dumb.

I used to run my life with a bazillion tabs open. I thought I had to be everything to everybody. To only eat organic, avoid plastic, practise yoga, meditate, strength train, play with my kids every day whilst also teaching them to play independently. And along with also keeping my home neat and tidy, being a complete sexual goddess as a single stay-at-home mum. I shouldn't forget, running a business, paying the bills and I haven't even mentioned a social life yet.

That's ridiculous.

I couldn't do it. In fact, I can't do it, so I stopped trying to multi-task and became something else . . . sound the trumpets . . . a passionate single tasker. What a relief.

Things now actually get finished. I can actually focus. Life feels so much smoother again and things are actually ticked off in the diary. It's a combination of lowering the bar to what you expect from yourself within a day and what you will allow to make you happy. To realise you can do anything you want in this life, but just not all at the same time.

Take my beautiful friend, Renee, from Purposehood. Legit, one of the best mums I know, and we like to keep it real, Renee and me. We have those talks. When Renee and I became really close, I was pregnant with my second babe, and Renee had two little girls. This woman out-mummed me on every level. Made most of their food from scratch, dressed like she stepped out of a dream and always had it together. Still, Renee felt the squeeze of life's demands and we often talked about the juggle and my marvel at not knowing how she did it all. Baby number three came along for Renee, the legendary, Tully, and with her husband working away the majority of the time, things started to get very real for her. Renee felt the weight of all the things and the biggest struggle I could see her have was the one with how she thought it would look vs how things were.

With Renee returning to work three days a week, something had to give.

For Renee, that was:

"The biggest change was to start choosing differently, sometimes.

Choosing meal prep over that extra few hours at the beach of a Sunday.

Choosing to ask for help over making it look like I had it *all* together.

Choosing store bought over home-made.

Choosing dry shampoo over a shower.

Choosing daycare over days with my mum.

Choosing done over perfect.

And choosing to let that all be okay. I had to shake off the belief I had to be and do everything for everyone, because I just couldn't do it anymore. It felt like I was failing. Feeling like I was always letting someone down was killing me. The hardest choice I had to make was choosing myself. I still get it wrong LOTS of the time, but I've made a start.

Working part-time and parenting three small children full-time is really fucking hard. But I'm open to things looking a little different these days and we're settling into our full, fun and slightly frazzled life together as a very busy family of five."

I know I've mentioned that Renee is my version of a Supermum. And I know the more children you add to the equation; the more things need to shift and change to accommodate a growing family. One of the biggest shifts that needs to be made is within our expectations.

"In my early days as a mother, I expected I could be my

children's whole world. And with Lola, my eldest daughter, I probably was. We did absolutely everything together, my little sidekick and me. Arlo came along, and I stretched to become the world for her too. Then Tully arrived, and my heart stretched again. But while your heart grows, your hand stretch doesn't. Nor does your time. I had to split my time between three children. Add in a household, my husband, and a career, the cracks started to appear.

These days, while I'm still there for all the important things and more, I've had to let other people step in to help. (So much love and respect for all the nurturing, patient and fun daycare and pre-school educators who hug, teach and show up for all the little people out there.) Sure, I didn't teach Tully the actions to *Twinkle Twinkle*, but those chubby little twinkling fingers don't look any less adorable held up over that smiling face.

I've also started getting a little real with my kids. They need to see their mum taking care of herself, spending time with friends, going on dates with their dad. They need to see that their mum can't be or do it all. And you know what, I hope my kids will see me being real with them as an invitation to do the same."

When doing less, gets you a more honest life with more real moments, that has to be a good thing, right? Quality over quantity always. Renee thinks so too.

"Slowly, I'm learning that by Marie Kondo-ing my to-do list and getting clearer about what it is I actually want that life is a little lighter.

There actually is room to do what I want. I just have to stop waiting for it to appear and choose to make it."

Don't you just love that?

It's always about the choices we make and where everything sits on the priority list.

Who is it helping

if you run yourself into the ground?

7.
THE STRENGTH IS IN THE SOFTENING

How many times have you heard people say, 'stay strong' or 'tough times don't last, tough people do'? Heaps. Let's just say you've heard them heaps. And look, I get it. I applaud strength. Strength is so important, but everyone's definition of strength is different. There is this completely outdated notion that to be strong you mustn't ever show emotion. You must be stoic, fierce, and heaven forbid, *even* afraid. There is such strength in actually softening. Becoming vulnerable and open to all the feelings and truths life has to offer takes courage, guts and all those other 'big and bold' feelings on the scale.

How does your definition of strength serve you?

Is there somewhere in your life where you feel you are holding back or holding things in, to stay strong?

When I first shared, after a lifelong dance with anxiety and living in the grips of fear for over two years, I wasn't sure how people would respond. Then after sharing on a worldwide stage—through my first book, *Becoming Brave*—that adding some medication to the mix helped to support me, it really stepped it up on the vulnerability scale. I'd spent a lifetime fighting my anxieties, running from them, battling them, ignoring them or believing I was broken because of them. The freedom and the softness that came with putting my hand up and sobbing in a heap to my doctor changed my life. Sharing that with whoever is listening is freeing.

Our truth, our complexities and our messy parts are the things that make us, us.

That's what makes us relatable.

That's what fosters connection.

I was walking with my friend, Lyndsey, yesterday and we began talking about anxiety. What started as a semi-serious discussion about the fear and overarching worries many of us live with ended with us in hysterics about the absurdity of it all. I shared with her that when I'm feeling particularly anxious or overwhelmed within my life; I take a little longer to lock the doors. It's like I really want to ensure I've seen they are locked so it's etched in my mind. If I worry about having locked the doors later I can recall I did actually do it.

Lyndsey said she does it in threes. "It's locked, it's locked, it's locked."

I burst out laughing because I do too. Lyndsey's friend used to do things in sequences of eleven! We threw hilarious stories of this back and forward for ages. I have taken pictures on my phone of power points being off. Lyndsey has made her mum drive over to her house to check *things*. My favourite story of all was a woman who always took her clothes iron to work with her, so she never had to wonder if she switched it off.

This woman is my hero.

She beat the system.

Through sharing our story with each other we softened, laughed at our crazy and realised we're not alone. #Winning!

> **Do you have any little quirks you do to feel safe?**

We all know anxiety shows up as a messenger to encourage us to look a little deeper. For now let's just have a chuckle at the weird, or perhaps, not so weird shit we do.

I love us.

When you stop avoiding your feelings and instead soften and lean into what is actually there for you, you unlock a deeper understanding of who you are.

When you stop fighting against yourself you get the opportunity to rest and soften.

When you soften you have way more chance of seeing things as they actually are.

When you understand more about who you are, you become surer of yourself.

When you are surer of yourself, you know you can handle anything life throws at you.

When you know you can handle all the love, loss, grief, confusion and anything else that life lobs your way, guess what? I'd consider that pretty effing strong.

A person willing to feel their feelings rather than avoid them shows strength. A person willing to open their heart is far stronger in their heart than when they decided they didn't want to risk it. And a person willing to learn from their mistakes shows more strength in themselves as a badass on the emotion-o-metre, as far as I'm concerned. Softening and being open to 'all life has to offer' takes a strength that can't be measured. Like so many things in life, trusting in your heart and the things you can't see invites you to draw from elements of yourself you would otherwise have likely missed.

Less force, more flow.

Less fight, more freedom.

Less control, more contentment.

Now if it's got to be a little more of some *things* and less of *others*, this list feels pretty dang good to me. If there's an area of your life where holding it in is no longer serving you, now would be a really great time to let it out. Connect with someone you trust and have a heart to heart. Write a letter where you process all the feels and get to a place of clarity and peace with whatever the situation is. Try not taking to social media and word vomiting it everywhere. There is always a time and a place for a public share, but I've seen many beautiful souls end up with regrets because they hit the socials with it all too soon. Before you ever share any personal story of any kind make sure you have 100% done the work around it. Ascertain your sense of self and your experience of the situation is not dependent on anyone else's perception of what you write or say.

So important.

The last thing you need is to take one step forward and three steps back because some douche responds with the sensitivity of a piece of sandpaper.

The

strength

is in the softening.

8.
IT'S NOT ME, IT'S YOU

Let me just say, some people are completely off. Like they are completely bonkers and not in the fun, Mad Hatter kind of way. Have you ever just looked at someone and thought, 'DICKHEAD?' Yeah, well, I have. I'm just going to throw this down. Some people are not very nice. Some people in this world don't care about others and some people are selfish.

These are not your people.

It's not your job to *fix* these people.

And if your path encounters one or more of these people, then I'm sorry.

It won't matter what you do, you'll be wrong.

It won't matter what they do, it will be your fault.

It won't matter how hurt you are, in their eyes, you deserved it.

Again, these are not your people.

The reason I think it's super-duper important to have a few pages dedicated to the fucktards of the universe is because it helps. It helps to know even though you have the best flipping intentions and you are a good person, and have a solid understanding of right and wrong, some people won't. And *that* is not your fault.

That is life.

That can happen.

They are assholes.

What you do with that information and the pages they hold in your story is entirely up to you.

Living a positive life doesn't mean you're not allowed to get pissed off.

You can *totally* get pissed off.

TRUST YOUR RAGE.

Rage has been the catalyst for some of my most pivotal moments, like, ever.

Anger shows up when you are passionate about something and that's been ignored. Your anger means *something*, so be sure to pay attention to its message.

> **Can you see a place where you are holding anger?**
>
> **How is it showing up for you in your body?**
>
> **Is it actually helping you to stay stuck in a toxic emotion?**

I'm especially aware of how anger feels within my body when it comes to my children and even more so when I was pregnant. My anger shows up to let me know that something or someone has crossed a boundary. I am Mumma, hear me roar—but, staying in a space that is so fiery is destructive.

Staying in this space of fury serves no one.

Get the memo, then delete the file.

Don't let dick-ish people keep your rage. Don't let them have your hate.

Feel it, then free it.

Hate is such a heavy emotion to carry, and it penetrates every area of your life. Even if you don't think it's with you, hate will seep in faster than water through socks on a wet doormat.

Feel it.

Acknowledge it.

Choose what you're going to do about it, then let it go.

Some people won't care if they hurt you and it helps to accept it.

You can't control them.

You can't control what's served up to you, but you can control what you're going to do about it and who you choose to have in your life because of it.

Some people will break your heart and waste your time.

Some people will take advantage of you and leave you high and dry.

Some people are liars, cheats and they will get what's coming to them.

What they create is their Karma, how you respond is yours.

I know these people are out there, but I still believe people are doing the very best they can. Even the meanies. Even the players.

Even the advantage takers. This doesn't mean it's okay, or that we need to allow them a space in our life. We can accept some people don't have our best interests at heart, and that, my friends, needs to be okay.

My dad has a saying I've heard many times over the years, especially in one instance where I held my tongue whilst seemingly being walked over. Or when I chose to not hold it in and let all my spiciest words fly and fall right into the baited trap. (Super classy.)

"Don't let them win," or a slightly different variation. "They've won."

This used to really bother me because I don't like to lose. No one does. The other day though, after losing my shizzle because I had every right to lose my shizzle, my dad said to me again. "They've won."

Well no, they didn't because I'm not competing with anyone. I wasn't put on this earth to prove myself right and them wrong. I don't mind being wrong. I'm sure my friends will attest to the fact I am the first to put my hand up and say, 'I f'd up,' or 'I could have handled that better.' That's usually when they say, 'No way G, let's roll out. I've got chu.'

I am not 'in it to win it'. I just try to ensure I speak my truth where possible and honestly make the decision that feels right at the time. Does that make the instances of encountering horrendous people any less? Nah. What it does do is set you free from the grips of knowing there's no right way to handle these people except the way that feels most right and true at the time. If you can *respond* rather than *react*, you will probably feel way better for it, but there's nothing wrong with a little colour if you feel that needs to be served up.

Upholding your loving boundaries is important. You can't do life in avoidance of these energy and life force vampires. They are undoubtedly a part of the human experience. Accepting they're a part of the story helps you understand both life and people are both beautifully and simply complicated.

I could add in here that hurt people, *hurt* people, but I'm fairly sure I'll cover that within these pages soon enough. We don't have to understand everyone. You don't have to find peace with everyone, but closure is a gift we give ourselves and in the words of Ariana Grande, "Thank you, next . . ."

Some people are fucktards.

Carry on.

9.

YOU'RE NOT WHO YOU WERE

At some point if we're paying attention, we realise we are our own greatest teachers. How that comes about for each of us is as unique as a snowflake. If we reflect on where we've been, where we're going, and take a good hard look at the signs before us, then we're in for one hell of a show.

I'm just going to come out and say I've had a blowout. I've popped a fender. Burst a floatie. Lost a pillow. In other not so funny words, my right breast implant has ruptured.

Fudge it.

In my superyacht days when I was twenty-seven, I began my two years of research that led to my decision to have the breast augmentation. I found an amazing doctor and flew from Canada to the USA where I allowed a surgeon to slice open my armpit. He took a scalpel to my pectoral muscle and slid a 300cc bag of silicone under the muscle close to my heart and set me up with a solid pair of breasts. I loved them. Although I was slightly embarrassed of them and often covered them up, initially I convinced myself it was a great thing I finally felt more in proportion, womanly and definitely sexier. But I always kind of felt like a little bit of a fraud. Like these two tenants weren't who they cracked up to be, but they were here, and I was determined to make the most of them.

Not so long ago, I started getting pain in my right boob. I put it down to life and the fact I was often wrangling one or two children at the weirdest of angles and I'd probably pulled something. The pain made my skin sensitive and often shot through my nipple. Then I found a lump, and I knew I had to sort it out. In the meantime, I read about implants a lot. I read about what's in them, about how you remove them and what side effects these fun bags can have on the body. It shocked me. Like seriously forking shocked. How could I have these in my body? How in the felafel did I think this was a great idea? What in the fork am I going to do now?

 Then I started to panic.

 My chest felt heavy.

I felt the full weight of the decision I made so flippantly that could have affected my health and quality of life. My doctor advised that go for an ultrasound pretty quickly. A few hours after the scan he called to say, 'You have a suspected rupture and I need you to come back and see me.' An appointment with a surgeon was made to have them removed followed by all the feels when I realised these tenants were being evicted.

 I've been scared for my health.

 I've been pissed at myself.

I've been upset about how they will look.

Confused at how I let this happen.

Angry for being so freaken vain.

Frightened for what this will mean for the boys while I recover from surgery and that is just the tip of the iceberg.

The thing is, I understand the rollercoaster of emotions, so I'm doing my best not to judge these thoughts, but to look at them with compassion and forgiveness. This growth game, it's always changing, there's always a new layer and a deeper level of understanding and connection that shows itself. We all have things we don't love about our appearance. We all have elements of our make-up and past that are zero fun to look at and this is the perfect example of an AFGO right here (Another Forking Growth Opportunity).

To feel chosen and appreciated in this life, which is a core value of mine, I have to appreciate myself (rolls eyes). To have a life filled with love, I have to love myself first. Like, completely, you know? In all my quirks. With all my lumps and bumps. With all my scars. In all my glory. I thought I was doing okay at this, but that's not how this works.

> In the words of Tracey McMillan, "You ask for patience; the universe will give you a line at the bank."

I'd walked right into this one.

So, how do I move forward and find the AFGO in this? First priority HEALTH always. I know this now; I know that my health is the most important thing I have, and silicone, out they go. Nope, they won't be replaced.

Second, how are they going to look after all this? Much like a deflated balloon, I guess. The first image that comes to mind is Magda from *Something About Mary* and her great set of knockers you see as she sunbakes topless. Google it. That's the vision I'm holding for them currently.

Third, who will want me now? *Cue the violins, Katie, I mean, come on now.*

Well, let's hash it out anyway. No one will love me the way I need to be loved until I learn to love myself in that same way first. Now, we all know the respect I have for myself is really way more important than a concern about finding a man, but you know, lady, that fear, thought and concern is real. It's there and I'm working through it. My rational mind is all like, *The man I wish to call into my world will love me for me and won't care that I can tuck my boobs under my armpits.* But the sensitive woman in me still harbours fear around the idea no one will accept me now that I can do origami with my breastage. I know I'm making light of the situation and I'm doing it because I know how forking ridiculous it all sounds. Fear is the ultimate neon sign for me for where I need to show up next and gift myself some healing. This is my work.

I am my own best teacher, just like you are your own best teacher.

I am not who I was.

> **Can you see where you no longer hold the same beliefs?**
>
> **Can you see where your priorities have shifted?**
>
> **How does that make you feel?**

I am not the woman who thought it would be a red-hot idea to implant domes of chemicals in my chest. I get mad at the entire thing, but I'm not who I was, I am the person who I have become because of her. The choices we have made before now will often be with us for the rest of our life. I know this choice will be along with truckloads of others, but let's not be mad at who we once were, because every choice we made at some point was the right one for us. We have no idea how it would all play out. Can we all just let that be okay? Like Tracey said, "You ask for patience; you get a line at the bank."

I asked for a love where I am chosen every day—not because I have to, but because I get to—and now I am the one who will gift that to myself.

Not because I have to, but because I get to.

I'm not who I was but

I am

the person who I have become

because of her.

10.
MAYBE THE BEST WAY FORWARD IS TO STOP

Girlfriend, I wish someone would have said this to me at one point or another. Actually, that's not entirely true. People have told me. My beautiful mentor, spiritual guide and cosmic revolutionary person, Lauren Aletta from Inner Hue, told me that back in autumn. When I was feeling a bit pressed and empty on the creation front she basically said, 'Babe, you know you need to rest now right? This isn't time to create, this is time to rest.' It still took me a few weeks to get the memo and stop pushing towards something I wasn't quite aligned with at that time. So, I spent my winter moments asking myself, 'What is it I'd really like to be doing right now?' Turns out, what I wanted to do was watch a shit tonne of *Downton Abby* and all of *The Crown*. For someone who would say they didn't like period drama, I would now call BS on that because I loved it. I became obsessed with it; it gave me exactly what I needed in terms of escapism and switching off my mind.

Every time I sat down to write this book—this epic little collection of ah-ha's you're now reading—nothing came out. I would create the time, but nothing flowed through like it usually would. I worried my words had dried up. What if *Becoming Brave* was to me like "Achy Breaky Heart" was to Billy Ray Cyrus prior to "Old Town Road"? What if I really was a one hit wonder?

Yeah, nah.

I just needed to wait.

> **Is there an area of your life where you're pushing and meeting resistance?**
>
> **Are you putting pressure on yourself and getting nowhere?**
>
> **Is it possible that this may not be the best use of your energy right now?**

We can't pour from an empty cup. I had given so much of myself to *Becoming Brave,* my book launch, a huge campaign, TV, radio and speaking events, all on top of the usual mum-ing that I was tapped out. I needed to embrace my internal winter and hibernate hoping eventually once all the inspo and self-care had been restored, the words would flow, and I'd feel all inspired and wordy again.

Wouldn't you know it, it worked.

Here I am, 10,000+ words in and I'm showing no signs of stopping, yet. Good thing though because that's still not even half-way done. What I've learnt is that it's okay to not be ready.

I walked a beautiful client of mine through this situation the other day. Let's call her Michelle. She was moving through some deeply emotional stuff. There had been some big losses in Michelle's life and the pull to up level her business was calling her. She has big dreams, lofty goals but was getting bogged down in the smaller details of making it all happen under the weight of the feelings swirling around inside her heart. She wanted to move forward. She wanted to share more. And she wanted to feel successful. It's easy to think the way to get ahead will always mean doing the big-ticket things that will propel you forward in life and business. That's the path, right? Maybe. What I suggested to Michelle was to pause. I offered her some words, 'Maybe you're just not ready yet. Maybe now is not the time to push forward but instead the time to be still and heal.' You could see the colour come back into her face and the weight lift from her shoulders. You could see that by giving herself permission *not* to be ready, she gave herself the space and confidence to do things her own way. I adore this woman and the way she continues to let it be what it is and do the flipping work. Even if it looks different to how she once thought. Even if it means moving through her *stuff*. And even if it means pivoting on her path, sometimes, the best way forward is to stop. Not forever. Not because someone tells you to, but because you know that it's what feels right for you even if you had already written it in your diary, made a few posts about it and told your grandma.

It's okay not to be ready.

It's okay to need to pause.

It's okay to not have the answers and be sad or mad or both.

Life is simply complicated like that, but when you know the path is always the path you'll always end up where you need to be. The only question is what choices you make in the meantime will dictate the state at which you arrive.

Strung out hot mess doesn't look great on anyone. Zen, Mega, Goddess, Wonder Woman; however, has *you* written all over it. You're a babe.

Pause.

11.

LEVEL UP

If you aren't singing that Ciara song in your mind right, then go search it and get the tune because I am *all* about it.

Level Up.

Level Up.

Level Up. Level Up. Level Up.

Personal growth is all about levelling up. Spiritually. Physically. Emotionally. Nutritionally. *Level Up.* You can also work on levelling up in your business, your relationships, your holidays—you name it. If you look at the big picture and just throw it on out there that you are want to 'level up' your life, that's not only super vague but incredibly daunting. If you want it to happen, get specific. All you have to do to level up in any area of your life is to look at how you can improve it *slightly*.

> **What's an area of your life that you'd like to level up?**
>
> **What do you think could be a realistic, fun, and achievable next step?**

It might start with your physical game. You might go from doing no exercise to two walks a week. You could go from doing three cardio sessions to adding in a strength session. Or you might start Pilates (which is where I'm at because I even look at a barbell and throw my pelvis out). #Athlete. You might invest in a PT once a week. The level up you choose is personal and relative to what you're actually doing already.

Nutritionally, you might level up by buying organic fruit and vegetables. Or by adding more vegetables to every meal. You might skip the packaged goods and cook from scratch. Maybe even make your own soups or broth. Or, prep on a Sunday. Perhaps, it's replacing soft drink with soda water. It's about looking for ways to lift your growth game, and lady, you're here because I know you want your growth game to be strong!

Business. How can I do this *one* thing better? Then the next thing and the next.

Relationships. What can I give to my partner or friend or mother to help them shine? How can I communicate more clearly with them, so they meet both our needs? How can I show my love for them today? Could it be no phones for you after 6 pm? Implementing a girls' or date night once a month? Whatever you feel would help improve your relationship then level up in that way.

I am no stranger to using the term: I'm feeling stuck. I've learnt it always comes before a period of growth and expansion. First, I have to feel uncomfortable within my life and in my skin and then a solution always reveals itself, and I'll commit to expanding in some way shape or form.

For me, creatively, I created a new membership group called *Brave Makers*.

Nutritionally, I am having a crack at fermenting garlic and honey to help us through the winter months. Physically, I went to a yoga and meditation class and by the way, I haven't had my butt on the mat for three years.

Small, simple and all upgrades.

Ask the same questions throughout your life as often as you feel called to. This is not about never being satisfied, because *y'all* know me, I love some appreciation for the moment we're in. This is about knowing that the destination needn't be where it stops. There's always room for new, there are always something to aspire to, and there are always ways to learn and reinvent your life in any moment you choose to do so.

Personally, I think that is forking inspiring.

There's always room for growth.

Level

up.

12.

FAILURE IS A FEELING, NOT A DESTINATION

Far out I have so many words swirling inside of me right now on this topic I feel like I might burst if I don't legit get them out of my body. I know an important topic like this when it lands because I get all tingly.

I *am* tingly.

I have spoken to thousands of women in my time around fear, and a real buzz kill of a fear for many is the fear of failure. How that presents itself is different each time, but here's the thing.

Failure is a feeling not a destination.

If you think about it, it's not the low-grade on your essay that scares you, it's the feeling of the new story that comes with it. It's not your business closing that kills you, it's the feelings that will bring up for you that scares the living daylights out of you and the story that you will have it mean, for you, and about you. Failure doesn't exist if you keep moving forward. You can momentarily *feel* you've failed, but unless that's where you unpack and live for the rest of your days, your personal disaster needn't be the biggest event in your life. You get to choose.

People flunk tests.

Businesses close.

Relationships end.

Doors shut.

Money gets lost.

We don't achieve the results we hope for. Events like these are not the end result. They are not the final station on the train ride that is life. They are all a part of the scenery and what a power-packed lesson they bring.

> **Can you see where you were more afraid of the story rather than the destination?**
>
> **How do you feel about this now?**

Not once did I see my relationship ending as having failed. It ended. It ended because it had to and that's what was best for all involved. Not everything is meant to last forever, in fact, nothing ever does. Now, I know that sounds like a massive Debbie-downer but it's not. It's freeing! Why spend your days white knuckling it trying to make everything you begin last for always when that's just not the way some things are meant to last? I'm willing to hedge my bets it's not the actual outcome that freaks everyone the F— out, it's the feelings that will come along with it that stop us in our tracks!

This realisation is something you can work with, right?

This is something you can use.

Feelings are just feelings.

They are messengers.

They are internal responses to external experiences.

That's *it*.

We are the ones who give it a meaning and a back story. I totally get there are some feelings that are super heavier than others and ones we want to avoid more than others. I get that, but if you attempt to curate your life by picking and choosing which feelings you want to experience more than others, it's indeed a slope and you're missing all the good bits.

You avoid the hurt; you miss the healing.

For. Reals.

Pain breads resilience.

If you continually try to miss the shit stuff in life, how on earth do you expect to learn to handle it when it inevitably comes knocking? Because it will. Not to mention the anxiety that would accumulate the more you try to do everything in your power to avoid feeling any discomfort. Far out. I've got a chest pain even typing that. I have a profound respect for our minds and our desire to want to control the outcome.

> Hot tip alert: As a recovering anxious mess, making friends with all of my feelings and releasing attachment to my experiences is the absolute shizzle. When you embrace all your feelings and make the choice not to judge them then, lady, you just scored yourself the keys to your castle.

Failure is a feeling, not a destination and once you take away the story fanning the fire, whilst being open to all your body's feelings, failure loses its power. To put it simply, it's just another side effect of human-ing and part of your beautiful story. So, next time that sinking feeling of failure comes up for you, get a little curious and see if it's the destination that worries you, or the bio you will add to your story because of it. Be open to experiencing all your feelings and quit playing favourites. Failure is a feeling, not a destination. Can we all just breathe a huge sigh of relief now?

    Game on!

You avoid the hurt; you miss *the healing.*

13.

IT'S GOING TO FEEL WORSE, BEFORE IT FEELS BETTER

I know this might sound a little sketchy, but I love how this works, like seriously, *love* it.

You know how people say that 'this will pass'? Well, girlfriend, it fully does. It might pass like a kidney stone, but everything eventually always does.

> Note: Not before it teaches us what we need to learn, and that, my friend, is the pot of gold at the end of your rainbow.

Most days my J O B title would say that I'm a writer and a coach. As you can imagine, writing is a solitary activity. Generally, day-to-day I see most of the same people—my kids and the preschool mums—who I adore, *ha*. The lather-rinse-repeat cycle of my life, while beautifully comforting and dependable, was feeling a little restrictive. Being the gal I am, I started feeling a tad isolated and quite possibly a bit sad. This was showing up as me rolling out some charming personality traits of being a tad irritable and possibly a little-lot of snappy-ness (bitchiness).

Every new level of our life will require a different version of us.

Every now and then we are called to step up.

Every vibe we put out into the universe registers and the mega babe that is the cosmos heard my cry and bloomin' oath she delivered.

Thanks to a few misaligned items in my timetable, I'd found myself without a place to work and requiring online access at a particular time. My home was out of action thanks to the painters who were doing an epic job. I was stuck. Stuck until I wasn't. Now I am writing this to you from my very first day at a co-working space in Newcastle, and just quietly, I am loving myself sick. I love everything about this space. I'm jazzed that there are people around me. I love that I have my own little 'hot desk' for the day and I love that I can work here once a week and I actually get to be a part of something. How epic is it that I get to see people and feel creative and there's a coffee shop next door. I even used my 'keep cup' for the first time, because I'm getting a coffee from somewhere other than my kitchen. I love that my friend, Amy, works at the front of the house and that places like this exist. How great is it that, that again, as always, the emotions of discomfort show up right before another growth opportunity. This feels so flipping exciting to me, I can't even express fully.

>I feel legit.

>I feel like I have a place to go.

I feel like I've got my big girl pants on (not to be confused with a full brief; although, I do have them on today because, responsible) and it feels really expansive.

I wouldn't be here if I hadn't had a gut full of my own 'set up' and if everything hadn't of appeared to be all cluster-fucky. Cluster-fucky-ness is often the gateway for the best solutions. Even when we doubt our *now*, it's always a part of the plan. Things go wrong to get our attention and every opportunity is a chance to look for a new way to be. For now, this is my next right step. All it took to figure out what that was, was for so many things to feel wrong.

> **Can you see an area of your life that feels stuck, stagnant or frustrating?**
>
> **Do you know there's a next step right there but you're just not sure how to take it?**

My beautiful friend, Renée Wilkinson, did, and it turned out to be the catalyst for the best career pivot of her life. Renée had followed the textbook path. She had a successful career in TV, was ticking all the boxes, a cracking but not so healthy social life, but something still just wasn't right.

She tells us,

"I felt like I was constantly hiding some part of myself. At the peak of barging my way down that *not* true path, everything was heavy and felt so jarring to my truth; where I lived (a huge, numbing apartment complex on six lanes of traffic in Sydney); the acquaintances I was trying hard to be friends with; the career I was pushing for (mainly to prove

I could be the youngest to do it); the guy I was dating. Socially, he was what everyone wanted, handsome, wealthy, doting, wanted to marry me and every time he brought it up I would wonder how soon it would be inappropriate to get a divorce. When I looked to the women further down this same career path I followed, I could see how my values for family, friends, work/life balance didn't align with the experiences I was witnessing through these women."

I asked Renée about whether it got harder before it got easier with such a huge realisation and transition.

"Yes and no. Once I decided I was done with that career path and knew I wanted to leave Sydney and travel, I mustered the courage to break it off with the guy. And a *huge* weight lifted off my chest. I felt free to live by my rules. The hardest part was battling with my ego. My ego really liked having the cool job, and the money and the parties. My ego didn't want anyone to know my *secret* of being intuitive, that would make me weird and an outcast, right?

I went travelling and, on my return, I had to go back and live with my parents, in my hometown, which was another decent ego blow.

When all the distractions peeled away, I had to face a lot of hurt that was being covered up. I had to build my new business from scratch. I had to keep deciding to not go back, and stick to my new path, even though the job offers (AKA money) and party invites (AKA ego boosters) kept showing up. But after a while, as I started to experience the freedom of being in my *Self* more and more, it became easier to walk my path. Not only that, I began to attract people into my life who became cheerleaders for my path. That was a whole new experience for me."

Trust played a huge part in Renée being able to change her course, but it wasn't always there. Like so many of us, we detach from our intuition and think our rational mind knows better. That's always until we realise our intuition is more powerful than we could ever have imagined.

Renée says,

"As someone who has been intuitive since a young age, I tried for a long time to block out the signs. I ignored the inner guidance so that my ego could create a persona I perceived would fit in easier with everyone else.

Side note: it did not, I made tonnes more authentic connections with the same people when I stopped trying to be someone else.

It took a lot of practice to lean into the fear surrounding the trust. But with baby steps it has now become second nature.

I got a Universal boot up the backside. There have been lots of little lessons on the way, but the biggest 180 was my sexual assault. Just prior to it happening, I mean a few hours before, when that man was close to me (we were in a social situation), I started to see a siren light. Like an actual flash of red light going off in my brain, but I pushed it aside. By this stage I was very well practiced at ignoring my intuition. Moments before the assault took place, as I was walking into the room where it occurred, I had every siren and alarm flashing in my mind screaming at me, *Stop! Stop!*

Stop! I ignored it and continued into the room. I didn't listen to the loudest most obvious signal the Universe/my Higher Self had ever given me and as a result; I went through a traumatic physical experience that flattened me down to ground zero and took years to rebuild. That experience will stay with me for many reasons and it has helped shape me into who I am today. But that moment just before, of being so egoic that I thought I knew better than the screaming sirens in my mind, that has humbled me deeply to trust."

These days Renée is without a doubt one of the most attuned, aware and soulful women I have the pleasure of being in orbit of. Her work as a Meditation Guide, Kinesiologist, Yoga Instructor, Intuitive and business owner is such a powerful force for good in this world. I am so grateful she is willing to share her experience with the world to help empower others.

She is the real deal.

Growth and change rarely come smoothly. It's like clearing out your wardrobe. It's going to look worse when your shit is all over your bed before you place it all back in there for easy access and a fresh new look.

Life.
Be good with a broom or
enjoy the mess.

14.
STOP LOOKING FOR THINGS TO FIX AND YOU'LL FIX EVERYTHING

In day-to-day life you will always get what you're looking for.

I don't mean the surface level stuff.

I mean the deep inner workings of things.

Let's say you are single and looking for a partner and you might say there are no great men left or no men anywhere. I'd ask you if that's what you believe, and you'd answer yes. And I'd be all like *ah-ha*, there it is. That's the belief you're holding and why you're getting what you're getting. Our minds are fluffing awesome at gathering evidence to support anything we want in this lifetime. Anything. Like the internet; you can find evidence to support any side of an argument you want. You choose what you're looking for and *bam*, confirmation.

The same thing goes for relationships. I'm not saying stick your head in the sand for the big issues because that would be crazy. What I am suggesting is that you take a breather from constantly being on guard. I'm talking about the issues you look for, reading into and result in you pulling a perfectly good thing apart because you're not comfortable with things feeling 'good'. The type when everything is cruising along nicely in your relationship and then you start second guessing yourself.

You read too much into everything your partner says.

You look for things that could be wrong and you assume the other person mustn't be happy because they didn't ask if you wanted the last chip.

You get what you look for and if you're looking for trouble, you will find it or most likely create it. If it wasn't there in the first place, you will most likely push a little too far and eventually upset them.

The thing is though, when I'm not looking for things that could go wrong there aren't any. When I stop looking for things to be okay, they automatically are okay. When I stop trying to micromanage every fluffing thing that could go wrong, I feel safer than ever.

> **Can you relate?**
>
> **Do you ever do things to avoid having to worry about them later?**
>
> **Do you ever just allow things to be and see how you'd move through a scenario by releasing control?**

One of the biggest things I have worked on and embraced is the ability to just 'be'. The ability to be content where I am and to accept it's okay for me to be happy with life exactly how it is and also allow it to be easy. *Farrrrk*. This was a challenge for me, and I spend most of my time honouring and redirecting my thoughts.

I also love a problem, or rather, I love to be ahead of the problem which explains why such a huge portion of my life I have experienced anxiety. I have always wanted to be ahead of the game and somehow worrying about the issue often gave me the feeling I was doing something productive towards solving it. I would even say I've been borderline OCD in spaces. Anxiety is all about control and a fear we have a lack of it. This desire to control or manage my surroundings shows up for me when I feel most out of control. When I'm nervous, I become concerned with whether I locked the doors or if the dryer is off. I also focus on washing my hands a lot because I don't want to have to worry about making anyone sick. It's like a protective thing I do to make sure I don't have to worry about a particular thing on top of my already beautifully busy brain. If you're looking for reasons the world may be covered in germs that will bring the loves of your life down, then friends, you will spend the rest of your life knee deep in Domestos with several packets of half-used antibacterial wipes in your purse whilst throwing around hand sanitiser like it's going out of style. #makeitrain None of that is a fun time, but I totally get the desire to want to look for the problem and beat it to the punch. We think by planning for all contingencies and by being extra prepared we will keep safe and relaxed, but actually it makes us antsy, a little neurotic and hello, anxious.

Stop looking for things to go wrong and assume everything is all right until someone says otherwise. It's not your job to read minds. It's not your job to micromanage everything. Today is the perfect day to resign as CEO of the universe and go about your business as if no one was up in your business at all. If handing over the reins and taking a step away from the micromanaged aspects of your life gives you a chest pain, I promise, it gets easier. You only have to do something once to feel just how great it feels to live a little lighter. You can trust yourself and the process a little more by choosing, wait for it . . . to trust yourself and the process a little more. Try checking things once as you leave the house. Consciously choose to look for the good in a situation where you'd drive yourself crazy with possibilities. Don't send the text that's asking for reassurance or validation from another. Then get out there and enjoy your day and celebrate the fact you just worked your willpower muscle like a boss! You get to choose who and/or what you give your energy to.

I hope you choose you and the situations where you can do something positive with it.

Today is

the perfect day

to resign as CEO of the universe.

15.

YEAH, NAH

Oh, I have been wanting to get to this chapter, radsters. I have a bit to say on this topic, so just a sec while I grab my soap box because I'm about to jump up on it.

Picture this. You have just started dating someone and they ask what you want for dinner and you don't want to seem too eager for a burger and chips, so you say indecisively, 'I'm cruisy, you decide.'

Errrrrrrrrnt. Buzzer sounds.

God forbid, you seem too eager for something. Now you end up with some Mexican catastrophe that you can't even eat but still you say *nothing*. What about at the workplace where you are in a meeting? Someone proposes a question but you reluctantly decide not to answer it because they referred to Suzie from

Accounting as 'bitchy' last week for daring to go against the big boss's idea. How about, you're going for a drive with your love when the topic comes up again about how you will school your non-existent kids? You totally disagree with sending them off to boarding school from kindergarten, but you don't say anything because you don't want to appear too forceful or the flip side, soft. Last time you had an opinion and wanted to discuss it further they called you 'hard work' and it ruined your entire afternoon.

Can you see where I'm going with this?

I mean, shiiiiiiiit. I know this scenario.

I mean . . . I. Know. It.

I have a lot to say on this and as you read it I want you to picture me on said soap box waving my hand in the air all street-like to make a point. Probably looks more like a royal wave because I've got no game.

Here goes.

Sharing your wishes doesn't make you 'needy'.

Having an opinion doesn't make you 'hard work'.

Standing up for yourself doesn't make you a 'bitch'.

This gets me right in the feels.

> **Is this ringing any bells?**
>
> **Can you see an area of your life where things may have turned out differently had you had the courage to use your voice?**

If a man, or anyone, says you're 'hard work', it's more than likely he's avoiding any real emotional work on his part. The technical term would be lazy AF—, but because I don't know him/them personally, I'm just going to take a guess. If someone says you're 'needy', this means they aren't willing to step up and do what it takes to meet your needs. If someone has a problem with you backing yourself or calling them out on their mistreatment of you by calling you a 'bitch', this is usually made by someone who is weak in their position and has run out of things to say.

Saying what you think is called a CONVERSATION.

A woman with a voice is POWERFUL.

Having a vision, believing, having a preference makes you forking INTERESTING.

Suppressing your best to avoid making waves when you can be as deep and mind-blowing as the ocean, is robbing the world of the complex, inspiring force that is YOU.

Shall we go into a few more? Why not, hey?

Being upset when someone hurts your feelings does not make you 'emotional'. It makes you a human being and more than likely, they're an asshole for upsetting you. Choosing to make substitutions to your meal at a restaurant does not make you 'fussy'. It probably means your gluten intolerant or choosing to avoid weird shit that any sane person wouldn't like. Your friend or date can piss right off because you can eat what you like, and you don't need that kind of negativity in your life.

There is a disclaimer here.

I'm sure it won't apply to you though because you're perfect.

Holding your truth back from the world does nothing except rob the world of the amazing person you are. If you don't show up as your full self in every aspect of your life that's important to you, then you will always end up feeling a little frustrated and misunderstood.

What you are holding back from the world, dulls the world.

How do you know what you're truly capable of unless you start? How are you going to feel completely loved unless you choose to show yourself completely? How are you going to connect with your people, if you don't show people who you really are? Yeah, I know why we do it sometimes. But, 'nah', it's not a great idea for us in the long run. If you have to 'pretend' to keep the peace, is it really worth keeping? If you have to stay silent to avoid making waves, is a lake really that beautiful? If you have to pretend not to love what or who you really love, are the people you're trying to impress really that important?

Yeah, I get it.

Nah, there're way better ways to go. After all, it's far better to be liked for who you are than loved for who you are not.

Sharing your wishes
doesn't make you needy.

Having an opinion
doesn't make you hard work.

Standing up for yourself
doesn't make you a bitch.

16.
IT'S NOT YOU, IT'S ME

One of the best things you can do is own your shit.

Own it.

Sometimes, you will be a bit of an asshole.

Sometimes, you will make mistakes, and say, do or be, the wrong thing for people.

That's all a part of the process.

YOU'RE HUMAN.

I don't know who started this urban myth of the 'correct path', but I'd like to have a little chat with them. The notion we are meant to go through life doing all the right things and never stepping out of line is preposterous. As people doing this life thing, we are born into this body without an instruction manual. None of us have a clue what we're doing. We're all just making it up as we go and hoping for the best.

I 100% have no idea what I'm doing most of the time, but I am also completely sure of myself throughout it. Again, that little algorithm right there is simply complicated.

The thing is and by now I'm guessing you're picking up this confusing but, oh, so powerful theme of this book. This life gig is not meant to make sense, it's not meant to always be easy and you will make a shit tonne of mistakes.

Yep, a shit tonne.

That's a legit measurable term in my world, also known as 'heaps'.

I still think I could have handled things better in some way most days. Except for yesterday. Yesterday was an exceptionally rad life day. Although, I did step in dog poo, but that didn't even dampen my spirits. Today though, already I'm cringing at something I said during a Live chat. It just came out all wrong, and it's not even bad, but I'm worried someone will misinterpret what I was trying to say and then *they* will judge me for it.

See what I did there?

Let's break it down.

It's not someone else who would be the problem here because everyone will interpret things differently, that's a given. I'm judging myself for not getting it right, or not getting my point across clearly and that comes back to a core belief of mine, that I'm not enough. Yeah, well, inner thoughts, *I am enough. I am soooo enough.* I might get my words twisted occasionally, but that doesn't make me any 'less than'.

So, if you don't mind, we will all carry on and what I say next will hopefully make you feel way better about yourself and this messy human gig we're living.

> **Can you see an area of your life where you need to take responsibility for your behaviour and your actions?**
>
> **Can you see how much better it would be to meet that with compassion?**
>
> **Is there an element of you that now feels so much more empowered by this ownership?**

You will balls it up.

You will sound like a fool sometimes.

And you will probably get into stupid arguments.

That's okay.

You will probably drink too much at some point.

You will wish you hadn't messaged that person.

You will stay in relationships longer than you know is best.

That's also okay.

You will swear when it's not ideal.

Raise your voice inappropriately.

And let someone or yourself down.

That's okay too.

You will feel a whole array of human emotions across the spectrum of feelings and that is all a part of the process. The quickest way to get clear on what living in alignment feels like is by slipping out of it, that's going to look how it looks.

There's no prize for getting through life with a squeaky-clean report card. No one will hand you an award for being an amazing partner or friend 24/7. That shoot does not exist.

What does exist is our ability to learn from our shoot storms and learn how to dress more appropriately for the inevitable downpour of WTF moments that will come our way as we journey through this rad series of events called LIFE.

The *only* reason I know white wine is not my friend is because of the hectic list of cringeworthy moments that have come my way as a result of imbibing it.

The *only* reason I know I need to work on being okay with uncertainty is because I have pushed so hard to get it, that everything fell through my fingers.

The *only* reason I know how to truly embody bravery is because I spent so many years living in fear.

It's our uh-oh's that give us the biggest ah-ha's. Embrace your mistakes. Taking ownership of our mistakes gives us a chance to course correct. Owning our mistakes puts us back in the driver's seat. If you are constantly blaming someone or something else for the way your life is, then you are saying you have no power and no control over how things will turn out. Don't be that person. Put your hand up, own your shizzle and give yourself the opportunity to use the path you've been on to end up somewhere even better.

    You know what to do, ladybug.

    You know what to do.

It's our

uh-oh's

that give us

the biggest

ah-ha's.

17.
THE FIRST YEAR AFTER THE ONE BEFORE IS THE HARDEST

I just had a birthday. Now, I know what you're thinking; I look so young for my age, right? *Thanks!* This one was a huge one for me. Not because of the age but because it was the first one after the year before. It's been twenty months, at the time of writing this, since my divorce. If you are doing the math, I am well and truly into the second year since, and everything feels like it's mine again. I'm not watching the calendar, so to speak, because I've recreated the holidays and life with one full lap around the sun already.

The first year after any great loss is hard.

Why?

It's because it's a year of 'firsts' where things will look a little different.

When I lost my daughter, Gracie, at fourteen weeks pregnant, that first year afterwards was really hard. Everything was as though it was time stamped.

I would have been *this* many weeks pregnant.

This was her due date.

This would have been her first Christmas.

Honestly, everything was tinged with sadness because I always felt like someone was missing.

Have you had to navigate life after loss?

Are you perhaps living it now?

Have you ever thought things will never get easier?

The same thing presented itself throughout my first year as a solo Mum.

This is my first Christmas as a single parent.

This is my first Christmas sharing the kids.

This is my first birthday alone.

This is Archer's first birthday without his dad.

This is my first time getting the presents ready alone the night before.

There's a lot to do as a single parent—any parent, really—and it's not the big things that get me, it's the little things.

The footprints got me at Easter.

After being so exhausted after wrangling two babies to bed the last thing I felt like doing was being a forking Easter bunny and putting powder footprints everywhere. I know that might sound a little grinchy but y'all, for me, that's where things feel heavy because I can't share the load. The second time around the sun though, I know what to expect and I have my own way of doing things, but that first year—wow—she packed a punch.

The first year following the *big* event is rough, so let's not pretend it's meant to be anything but. What I do know is that it will pass and with that comes confidence and a knowing that you can do hard things. For us, I know this to be true. We navigated those first 365 days as best we could as a little wolf pack and I'm really glad we've past it.

A calendar year and all the hopes we hang on the days that go by are brutal while you're moving through something. I have no follow-these-steps-advice for getting through something like this, except to allow yourself to feel all the feels. Grief, loss and change are inevitable. That's a part of life and as beautiful spirited souls having a human experience, it's bound to be that way.

You can't put a time stamp on grief.

You can't choose when to be sad and when to unravel.

Sometimes you just need to feel the way you're feeling until you don't feel that way. If you try to avoid the hurt, you are for sure going to avoid the healing and isn't that what we all want. We are all cruising around with training wheels on in this life gig of ours. Personally, I don't think they ever come off. We're here to learn and here to make a difference. We get to choose if that's a positive one or not.

Let me share with you I've learned about the year before.

You can't rush it.

You can't prepare for it.

It's better if you don't judge yourself.

It's okay to ask for help.

It's okay to cry in front of people.

It's okay to not want to cry at all.

Get IN your feelings.

You can still be unbelievably happy, you deserve that.

If it's not okay today, then there's a good chance it might feel better tomorrow.

We can do hard things.

I love lists.

Elizabeth Gilbert always has such beautiful things to say about grief and loss. After losing her partner, Rayya Elias, to an incredibly aggressive pancreatic cancer, she posted these words,

> "People keep asking me how I'm doing, and I'm not always sure how to answer that. It depends on the day. It depends on the minute. Right this moment, I'm okay. Yesterday, not so good. Tomorrow, we'll see.
>
> Here is what I have learned about Grief, though.
>
> I have learned Grief is a force of energy that cannot be controlled or predicted. It comes and goes on its own schedule. Grief does not obey your plans, or your wishes. Grief will do whatever it wants to you, whenever it wants to. In that regard, Grief has a lot in common with Love.
>
> The only way that I can "handle" Grief, then, is the same way

that I "handle" Love—by not "handling" it. By bowing down before its power, in complete humility.

When Grief comes to visit me, it's like being visited by a tsunami. I am given just enough warning to say, "Oh my God, this is happening RIGHT NOW," and then I drop to the floor on my knees and let it rock me. It's a full-body experience. To resist it is to be brutalised by it. You just bow down—that's all you CAN do—and you let this thing roll through your heart and body and mind, in all its vehemence.

How do you survive the tsunami of Grief? By being willing to experience it, without resistance. By being willing to feel everything. And being willing to accept the unacceptable."

As always, however you feel is right on time and the best way out of something is through.

Without

resistance.

18.

TRUST YOUR GUT

Intuition. It's everything.

I don't make a move in life without feeling into it—intuitively.

It's a very feminine way of doing things.

Living by your intuition is not for the fainthearted. Trusting in something you can't see is righteously brave and I'm not going to lie, takes a little practise. Not because you 'have to get it right', because you don't. It's about learning to *lean in* to that which you can't see and quietening your rational mind that wants to deal in facts rather than feelings. Your rational mind loves a planned path. Your rational mind loves a textbook approach and the path well-travelled. It loves to vibe on what Janet from Accounting would do or what Susan down the road says is best. It definitely has a lot of your parents' favs thrown in and leaves very little room for *feels*. It rarely celebrates your sense of knowing but prefers your ever-calculating brain. How's this though, it's been said that our gut is like a second brain?

Say whaaaaat? I KNOW.

Now it's not just me and some totally woke friends sitting around drinking chai and shooting the breeze bringing this stuff up. This is legit. There are plenty of studies out there supporting this and documentaries on the mind-gut connection and the gut's ability to impact anxiety and depression in those experiencing it. Our body is made up of energy, everything is energy, and everything has its own frequency. We respond to each other's energy subconsciously without us having to do anything about it. We respond to a room's energy, the energy of an email, a phone call, time in nature, the energy of the beach, it all impacts us in some way. We read and respond to it whether we acknowledge that fact. This is what chemistry with another person is. It's that whole, 'my atoms like your atoms' type of thing. While I don't nor do I really want to understand the entire science behind it, the magic within it I completely get.

I know that it's our compass.

I know that it's our true north.

And it will always, always, always know the way.

You will know the truth by the way it feels.

If you find yourself in turmoil or shrouded in anxiety over a situation or question, it's usually because you are trying to rationalise an answer rather than feel into it. You will know the truth by the way it feels. Every time. When you get out of your head and into your body, you will know what to do. Think about it. That voice telling you to not put your computer near some water, and you do it anyway, and that feeling comes over you like *'Guuuurl, you had better pick your computer up?'* That's your intuition.

The voice telling you that you really shouldn't say what you're about to say because you can feel that wave of *'Oh shit'* come over you? That's your intuition.

The vibes that this guy might be full of crapola.

Intuition.

The sense that there might be something more to the story.

Intuition.

The feeling that something keeps crossing your path because it might be a really great thing for you to acknowledge.

Intuition. Intuition. Intuition.

Where in your life have you felt your intuition communicate with you?

When have you ignored the vibes, and everything went to crap?

Where have you listened to the 'feels' and had everything pan out magically?

How do you think you can trust yourself more?

It's not always about the giant sweeping feels, sometimes it's really subtle. For me, I've learned to recognise these whispers through reflection. When I've ignored one of these little whispers, something has gone wrong. I'm left standing there shaking my head with the *I knew I should have listened* soundtrack playing over and over like a Bryan Adams song.

If you aren't familiar with the idea of trusting your intuition, there's no better time like the present to feel into which option is right for you. It's as simple as getting *still*, asking the question and running yourself through your options. The solution or option that feels lighter, more expansive and *right* within your body is the way to go. There's no need to seek outside of yourself, just come back to yourself.

What seems to bring most of us unstuck with making choices is the notion there is a right answer and a wrong answer. The idea of us making a mistake is one of the fastest ways to paralyse a person. First, there is no right or wrong choice. Just options. I am sure I'll say it several times before this book ends, but I want you to know that our path, is always the path. Like, you can't screw it up. Your path *is* the path. That's as simple and as complicated as you choose to make it. Second, read the first point again. I didn't really have a second point, but I really mean the first one, so, yeah.

> Glennon Doyle once said, "The most revolutionary thing a woman can do is NOT explain herself." I for shizzle agree.

Your intuition doesn't have to make sense to anyone else but you. Your feels are there for *you* and *you* only. There's something really powerful in being able to trust in that which you can't see.

So how do you know when your intuition is speaking up and when it's anxiety or fear taking over? Such a good question, you're a really bright spark, friend. Your truth and your highest good, AKA your intuition, will feel expansive, safer and almost like a sense of relief when you feel into it. A fearful train of thought or our good pal anxiety when leaned into will feel restrictive, fast and that fear will amplify. You'll want to run; it will often lead to more fear-based thoughts and so the cycle continues.

You will know your truth by the way it feels, and that is one beautifully trippy reason that we can always trust our gut. Don't you just love that?

You will know the truth
by the way it feels.

19.

I'M NOT HERE TO PLEASE ANYONE, THANK YOU

I was ready to share a post to Facebook last night. As I was about to finish it I paused and questioned if the last sentence would offend anyone, or would some people unfollow me? So, I sat with it because I've learned not to rush these things. Was it my intuition telling me to slow my row because this wasn't a great idea or was it a fear of being judged causing the hesitation? *Fear of being judged or rejected for the win.* Yeah, okay. I get that, but this won't do. Immediately I realised this was an old story and so circa 2015 that I posted it and felt really good about it and didn't check back in for a while.

The post went something like this:

'There's something to learn from every person you meet.

Look up from your phones, smile to your left, ask questions

to your right and see how different your experience is.

The person on stage may be the reason you entered a room, but the person you learn the most from might just surprise you.

P.S. I get that this might trigger some people. But if you ever walk into a room and think you're the most interesting person there, then you're either in the wrong room or a bit of a dick.'

It confirmed something, yet again.

I am not here to please anyone. I've no interest in pleasing people if it goes against my values, my morals, or what will support my family or me in living our best lives. I am also not interested in breaking rules or rebelling just for the hell of it. If it's important to me, that's a different story and an idea for another chapter, so stay tuned.

> **How would you move through your days if you never looked for approval from anyone else?**
>
> **What would you give yourself permission to do?**
>
> **Is there anything you'd do differently?**

What I know for sure is that my sense of self is no longer linked to the opinions of others.

Nope.

Not a bit.

My self-love game is strong.

I know that because it was tested on my walk with Oaks this morning as I was listening to a podcast and the conversation I was enjoying took a turn. They started talking about something that five years ago, or even one year ago would have potentially ruined me. It would have sent me into a spiral of fear and worry but today it went so differently. Today, I heard the words and for a minute I had to double take on what I had just heard. My tummy didn't flip. And my heart didn't sink. My mind tried to go there and follow the old thought pattern, but my mood didn't change. Their words no longer affected me because my sense of self has absolutely nothing to do with anyone else. It's all on me. I am finally aligned with approving and even loving myself as I am and I'm okay with however that looks.

'What does that look like?'

Saaaah glad you asked.

I validate me.

I am whole as I am.

I don't put anything out into the world until I am 100% sure I love it and I won't be rocked if someone else doesn't.

I try not to take things personally.

And basically, I have done a shit tonne of work on loving myself—read: accepting myself—as I am.

When you have been rolling around, doing this life thing looking for approval from others and seeking external validation for the things you do, you are setting yourself up to be downright miserable. If you feel people are always letting you down, I want you to look at something. What are your intentions behind the action? Say you agreed to organise the food for a friend's birthday. You put in loads of effort and you don't feel that your time and energy was acknowledged in the way you would have hoped. How do you react?

A) Do you carry on with your day and just hope they enjoyed the party?

B) Or, do you mentally start thinking about how you were wronged and how no one ever appreciates all you do? Also, about how you would never disrespect someone like that, and this will be the very last time you put yourself out there for them or anyone else for that matter.

I have been both people, so I get it. If you were all about answer B, chances are your expectations for helping out were that they would acknowledge you, and possibly praise you. This would deliver the validation you require to make you happy and fuel the cycle for external validation.

I get it.

The difference is if your intentions for supporting your friend and her party were purely about her having a good time. This makes you feel good and you know it's a great thing to do. You validate yourself; you don't give anyone the power to ruin your day or take the good deed away from you, and everyone can sleep a little easier.

It's a win-win.

See the difference? It's huge.

When you get clear on your intentions for doing anything and release the expectation for anyone else, you win all the games because you're only up against yourself. Expectations cause so much angst, I shit you not. Expectation vs Standards are very different but perhaps that's a whole other chapter again. Ha! Look at me making all these new chapters from this important one. The thing is though, it's all linked. You work on one area of your life and naturally it flows over into other areas.

Part of not being here to please everyone is knowing that it's okay to piss a few people off. The word 'no' might make them mad, but it will also set you free. Every time we say 'yes' to someone or something else that doesn't align with how we are feeling or want to feel, we are saying a big fat FU to our soul. We are saying 'your happiness is more important than mine' and if you're looking at being okay with who you are then this is a giant kick in the vag.

Side Note: I have not been kicked in the vag recently. I have carried two babies through Symphysis Pubis Dysfunction though. I assure you it's as unpleasant as it sounds and the two feels remarkably similar. Sooooo, yeah.

Being okay with who you are and what you do are two very big steps in the right direction of inner contentment and a way more fun experience. I can't promise you that you won't upset a few people with this new sass-packed version of your fine self, but I can with all certainty say that you will have way more fun doing it.

Sass for the win.

Saying, 'No', might make them mad, but

it will set you free.

20.

BLAME. WHEN YOU BREAK YOUR OWN HEART

I will go out on a limb here and probably trigger people who are still stuck in the blame game. I dare say more often than not *we* are the ones who break our own heart. Even though it feels really good—in the moment—to blame someone else, we have to take ownership of both the great things and the dodgy.

Now, I know there are some circumstances that are out of our control and completely traumatising events that can occur in life. I am not talking about acts of violence. What I am talking about is the situations where we go against ourselves, our heart, our judgement and by doing so, break our own heart. If you are ready to heal and free yourself from the hate and torture of blaming someone else, then you will have a whole array of lightbulb moments within this chapter. If you're not, then sweets, maybe skip this chapter but know it's here for you whenever you're ready to dive a little deeper.

> Is there an episode, or five, where you can feel already that you caused your heart to hurt much longer than need be?
>
> Do you positive think your way out of situations and avoid seeing what's actually there?
>
> Have you fallen in love with or date potential which only ends up hurting everyone involved?
>
> Do you believe things will get better?
>
> Do you believe you aren't enough and don't deserve better?
>
> Do you lack the confidence to be without them even though it's toxic?

I have broken my heart with my behaviour, reactions, stories and decisions more often than I care to admit. Acknowledgement is the key to moving through, though, right?

Right.

So glad you agree. I knew we were going to be friends. Here are a few of the classic moves where we are actually harming ourselves.

We stay longer than we should.
Ladies raise your hand if you've stayed in a relationship way past its expiration date. I'm picturing a sea of the emoji with the little arm going right up in the air.

I have. I wholeheartedly have.

Why do we do it? I mean, how long is a piece of string? I could go on, but I think you get the gist. Yes, partners or friends may treat us poorly or have wronged us in some way but ultimately the decision to stay and tolerate what we do is completely on us.

If that triggers you, there's your work. Blaming someone else for how you feel will only get you so far. But acknowledging your heart is your own, and you say how you will feel is the wild card entry to the grand final baby.

We act over our intuition.

Duuuuude. I feel this. I feel this in my entire body, and I could kick myself for all the times I let my ship run aground. Every time something has gone wrong within my life I am 100% sure that it's when I went against my intuition.

Every. Dang. Time.

The thing is though, I've learnt to make peace with it. Yes, I broke my own heart. Yes, some of my decisions will impact my life for the rest of my days. And yes, I regret some things but on the flip side, there're no accidents. I'm also *not* going to beat myself up—*anymore*—for not knowing what I didn't know or not understanding the impact and the sovereignty of that little voice or feeling. I didn't know the impact, because I didn't know the impact.

Now I do.

Onwards.

We don't forgive ourselves.

We can truly break our own hearts by carrying around the weight of things that aren't actually ours to carry. And we can be such assholes to ourselves when it comes to shame or guilt.

Why, though, I want to ask you, why? Personally, I have a massive bone to pick with whoever put the notion out there that we had to get things right all the time. I have punished myself so heavily for some of the choices I've made. I've spoken so harshly internally and diminished my light in more ways than I can count. And I've run from and avoided feeling all the feels which pretty much is just a distraction from doing the work.

It was always, always, always going to be messy.

If it wasn't for the pain and the hurt, how in the bejeezels could we get the courage and foresight to heal? I've said it before, and I'll say it again: We need to lower the bar for the expectations we have for this life thing we're doing. No one will award us a medal at the end for doing things a certain way. This leads me to the conclusion our experience is exactly what it's meant to be. Wishing it away won't change things. Saying it shouldn't have happened to you is arrogant. I know because I've said that. The famous *why me?* Which if your growth will allow it leads into *Why not me? Why should it be someone else instead of me?* And then you understand and level the playing field.

Happy to have you back.

By carrying around regret and shame and refusing to work through it and feel it *all*, you are robbing yourself of the healing and that doesn't have to be complicated. Feel the full force of the memory and see what lesson is in it for you. Feel it until you can navigate it out to the other side. Then when you understand why it was there and things had to be that way you can move forward.

You're welcome.

We blame someone else.
Seriously, though. By blaming someone else for how you are feeling, you are saying you don't have the capacity to heal yourself. Stop doing that. It's silly.

We focus on the wrong thing.

What are you looking for in that text?

What are you searching for in their words?

What are you gathering evidence to support in your life?

If it's not positive and for the brighter side of life, then you are breaking your heart on the daily, or at least impeding its healing.

I get how important it is to see the facts. I know how crucial it is to feel your anger. I completely understand what it's like to feel like you can't forgive them. But sweetheart, forgiveness has very little to do with the other person, and everything to do with severing the tie that holds your hate and rage to them.

> You get what you look for, angel face.
>
> Open heart, big fucking fence.
>
> Open the gate accordingly.

Blaming someone or something else is like giving someone the keys to your car and still expecting to drive. To take charge of your life, your healing and your future, look at what was, understand it for what it is. Then decide how you will carry on and be the person you want to be. You are far too much of a miracle to allow someone else such a large piece of your puzzle. I hope it's starting to feel like a brand-new picture.

When we blame others,

we break our own heart.

21.

REMOVE THE WORD 'JUST'. IT'S LAME

Y'all know I'm about to serve this one up on a platter. 'Just' is now one of those words I try to remove from my vocabulary whenever it appears. Every time you use 'just' it either looks like an attempt to lessen the impact, cushion the blow or quite frankly undermine your authority.

'I didn't mean it, I was just . . .'

'I'm sorry I'm late, I was just . . .'

'I know you are hurt, I just thought . . .'

Yeah. NO.

When we serve it up in a work capacity:

'I was just thinking . . .' holds way less power than, 'I was thinking . . .'

'This was just an idea I had . . .' is small compared with, 'An idea I had . . .'

You see where I'm going with this? The word 'just' is the ultimate downplay and lady, please, please, please, don't make yourself small for anyone.

> Is there an area of your life where you dim your light?
> Is there an area of your life where you are playing small?
> Taking the word 'just' out of your vocabulary is small but mighty, do you feel you can do that?

There is a lot happening in terms of levelling the playing field in these times we are in and I know change is coming. I was reading a post from Elizabeth Gilbert—can you tell I'm a fan? —a few days ago and honestly, the behaviours and requirements deemed necessary, and what's worse, the fact they were actually a part of our not so distant history, blew my fluffing mind. Here's the post:

> "In 1974, my mother tried to open a bank account in the state of Connecticut. The bank officer told my mother—who had ALWAYS worked outside the home, and who had been supporting herself financially since she was fifteen years old—that it was illegal for her to open a bank account in her own name without her husband's consent and signed permission. That happened in recent, living memory, people. That happened the year I started school. Just last week I spoke at a conference for the National Association of Women Business Owners—an organisation founded in 1988, back when it was still illegal for a woman to get a business loan without a man's signature on the documents.

That's also recent history.

Here's some ancient history: In ancient Rome, a woman would be arrested if they caught her walking around the city alone with money in her pockets. (How is that any different from what my mother faced in 1974?)"

"These are some of the stories I'm thinking about today. What I'm saying is this: For most of history, it's been illegal for a woman to be free in any way. Her body didn't belong to her, her labor didn't belong to her, her money didn't belong to her, her voice didn't belong to her. Certainly, her government did not belong to her.

In 1776, Abigail Adams wrote a famous letter to her husband John Adams, begging him "to remember the ladies" as he was creating this bold new American government. She asked that women's concerns be included in the conversation. His response was to completely patronize her and dismiss her. He said, "I cannot help but laugh." He said, "You are so saucy." He ridiculed her, but the patriarchy is no joke. It is deep, old and strongly invested in keeping its power. But the patriarchy is crumbling. Even in my lifetime, women have made extraordinary strides. But we aren't done. We will rise higher. And the patriarchy is kicking back right now against women with an ugly vengeance—the way dangerous beasts always kick when they are cornered. It will get uglier. Then it will get better. Because we will make it better."

Holy shit balls.

I feel this; I feel it with every fibre of my being, and we are here, and we will not downplay our words, our actions and our place alongside what matters to us. The word 'just' doesn't need to sit with us anymore because we don't need to share our views as an afterthought.

We won't *just* sit over there.

We won't *just* let you handle things.

We won't sit at the table *just* because it's the right thing to do.

We will take a seat at the table because it's our right to be there.

>BOOM! How's that for saucy?
>
>Bat-er-up!

We won't sit at the table just because it's the right thing to do.

We will take a seat at the table because *it's our right to be there.*

22.
EVOLVE OR REPEAT

I don't like to make the same mistake twice. I like to make it a whole truckload of times to really drive the lesson home. I'm an optimist so I have been known to talk my way around a situation many, many times. I like to call this 'when positive thinking goes bad'. Many would say, including Albert Einstein, not that I could find proof, the definition of insanity is doing the same thing over and over and expecting a different result.

Optimist – Insane = Potato

Far out. That doesn't really translate that well in the written word. Moving on. If you keep doing the same shit over and over and expecting a different result, you're kidding yourself. Realising that though can be a real fork to the eye and *then* once you've realised your pattern, you've got to do something about it. #buzzkill

> **Where in your life could you benefit from a new way of doing something?**
>
> **Are you ready to actually try it?**

I was working with an amazing woman this year who was getting really down because her ex kept contacting her whenever he was lonely. Not only did this keep her on the conveyor belt, it never allowed her to fully move forward. He would pop up and say he missed her but would never do anything about it. We have a word for dudes like him and let me tell you, it's not 'catch'.

Conclusion: What she was doing wasn't working. She tried deleting his number. She tried changing his name to 'don't answer'. What she really needed to do was block him. Block him from all the social channels, block his number and end the merry-go-round. This felt huge. This felt big. This was the only way.

If you want a different meal, make a different breakfast. There isn't another way to play that card. When it comes to getting over someone the delete and block works. It's a breath of fresh air. You don't have to worry t every time the phone rings you will have the rug ripped out from under you.

Now on the subject of break-ups or deleting and blocking, let me ask you this, if you don't want to do it and you have broken up, why?

Is it because you think he will eventually want you back?

Don't be the girl waiting around for the call.

Is it because you don't want to upset him?

Um, yeah, nah. It's time to protect your emotional wellbeing.

What if his house is on fire?

I hope he would have the common sense to call the fire brigade first. You don't want to be the person he calls to whinge about how his favourite Nickelback T-shirt smells like smoke and his Nintendo 75 got destroyed. What. A. Shame.

If it's not working for you, evolve or you will keep repeating the same situation, over and over.

Same thing goes for something that's triggering you. If something is bothering you in this lifetime have the courage to dive a little deeper with it and do the healing work around it. See things in a different way, move past it or keep repeating that same pattern. There's always an area of our life where growth is knocking.

The other day, I was looking up facts about bees to share with my son. I came across ten fun facts about bees for kids or something like that. I started reading, and it was like my brain pinged. It was overjoyed to be learning something new. It was like *holy shit, this is new information guys, we are forking learning!* This is great, make some room up there friends because here comes some knowledge. It was like a party in my brain and that was the signal that ah-ha, it's time to learn again. I'm ready to grow a little more.

When Archer was around two-and-a-half-years-old, I thought about doing another course, but my brain was full. I couldn't even ingest another sentence. There was no room at the inn. My brain did not ping, it clunked shut every time I tried to absorb something new. Donk. You've got to pay attention to your seasons but if your soul is saying put your foot on the gas, you have two choices. You can either be the one in the back saying, 'perhaps we should pull over and ask for directions'. Or you can be the badass who takes the wheel and says, 'hold on bitches we will see where this new road takes us'. One of those women will have way better stories to tell when they're older let me tell you.

I hope I'm at the nursing home saying inappropriate things to anyone who'll listen and explaining what the wrinkled tattoos I have used to look like before they all collapsed in on themselves. Then I would swear a bit, talk about what a catch I used to be, pick my saggy boobs up off the chair and play a game of bingo with some Kahlua in my coffee. I sound fun. I bet I get great at cards too.

If we aren't growing and evolving, we're staying still. If we're staying still, we're gathering dust. Gathering dust scares me a lot. Contentment I adore but dusty and on the shelf, you can have that.

Evolve or repeat.

It's okay to grow and change.

It's okay to want to do and be more.

It's okay to not have to do it all once.

But if there's something you wish to change then, sweet potato, the answer is clear.

Evolve. Or. Repeat.

P.S In case you wanted to learn what I learnt about bees; here it is. Don't say I never did you a solid. Facts about honeybees:

1. *Honeybees are super-important pollinators for flowers, fruits and vegetables. This means they help other plants grow. Bees transfer pollen between the male and female parts, allowing plants to grow seeds and fruit.*
2. *Honeybees live in hives (or colonies). They divide the members of the hive into three types:*

Queen: One queen runs the whole hive. Her job is to lay the eggs that will spawn the hive's next generation of bees. The queen also produces chemicals that guide the behaviour of the other bees.

Workers: these are all female and their roles are to forage for food (pollen and nectar from flowers), build and protect the hive, clean and circulate air by beating their wings. Workers are the only bees most people ever see flying around outside the hive.

Drones: These are the male bees, and their purpose is to mate with the new queen. Several hundred live in each hive during the spring and summer. But come winter, when the hive goes into survival mode, they kick the drones out!

3. What are these buzzing bugs most famous for? Delicious **honey!** But did you know they produce honey as food stores for the hive during winter? Luckily for us, these efficient little workers produce 2-3 time more honey than they need, so we get to enjoy the tasty treat, too!

4. If the queen bee dies, workers will create a new queen by selecting a young larva (the newly hatched baby insects) and feeding it a special food called **"royal jelly"**. This enables the larva to develop into a fertile queen.

5. Honeybees are fab flyers. They fly at a speed of around **25km per hour** and beat their wings **200 times per second!**

6. Each bee has **170 odorant receptors,** which means they have one serious sense of smell! They use this to communicate within the hive and to recognise different flowers when looking for food.

7. The average worker bee lives for just five to six weeks. During this time, she'll produce around a twelfth of a teaspoon of honey.

8. The queen can live up to five years. She is busiest in the summer months, when she can lay up to **2,500** eggs a day!

9. Honeybees are also brilliant boogiers! To share information about the best food sources, they perform their '**waggle dance**'. When the worker returns to the hive, it moves in a figure-of-eight and waggles its body to indicate the direction of the food source. Cool, huh?

10. Sadly, over the past 15 years, colonies of bees have been disappearing, and the reason remains unknown. Referred to as 'colony collapse disorder', billions of Honeybees across the world are leaving their hives, never to return. In some regions, up to 90% of bees have disappeared!

This was taken directly from National Geographic Kids and it's packed full of cool info on there in case your brain pings too www.natgeokids.com

Evolve.

Or.

Repeat.

23.

FACT OR FEELING

Today, I sat down with one of my greatest friends and I watched her torture herself. She wasn't sticking forks in her hand or anything like that, this was far worse. I could see her breaking in front of me. This was Mumma guilt, and it was coming from the stories my amazing friend, Renée, was telling herself. Her babes had started daycare for the first day and it got all her feels swirling around. That step is hard. I knew how she felt because my littlest love would have overnights with his dad soon. And let me tell you, the places that your mind wants to take you aren't always friendly.

Let's call my friend, Rhonda. Her name is actually Renée, and she's the greatest Mum on the planet and rad AF— but in case she doesn't want me using her real name we will call her Rhonda.

Rhonda arrived and straight away she was in her feelings. She was all up in them. Tears, big puffy nose and feeling everything. After a while, I asked her what the bottom line was and what was the story going through her mind to create all this hurt.

"I'm a bad mum," she answered.

She knew it wasn't true, but that's what was coming up.

"It's the end of this phase of our life. I'm not ready to leave my babies."

Now this is where I stepped in and was all like, woah, woah, woah, girlfriend. I knew this was not true.

"You are not leaving your babies, you will go to work for a few hours, three days a week. This is a job you will love, and you will support your family in a whole other way. This is not the end of the baby phase. This is an addition to your wonderful life. It's not a closed door, it's an open door and it can mean many wonderful things when you're ready to see it that way."

First you need to feel all the feels, then you need to look at the facts.

> **Where in your life right now are you projecting your feelings on to a situation?**
>
> **Did that actually happen or are you dealing in feeling?**
>
> **Take the emotion out of it and look at it in facts.**

Feeling vs fact.

Both are super important, and both play a valuable role in navigating anything heavy or anytime they conflict your head and heart. If you are up in the feels zone, it's usually a story you have attached to the situation.

'He ended things with me because he didn't think I was good enough...'

Did he actually say that to you?

Did he actually use those words?

If he didn't, lose the background story and take it for what it is. He ended things for whatever reason. That's okay. He's not your person.

'I have ruined my life. I drank way too much last night and embarrassed myself. People will be talking for weeks...'

Yeah, nah.

You may have had a few too many but the only person who's judging you is you. Deal in *fact* and the rest is all noise.

'I am a terrible mother because I have to put my babes in day care.'

F to the 'No' on this one.

Your babes will be well looked after because they are way too young to stay home by themselves. You need to go to work, you know, to feed them and keep a roof over their heads.

FACT.

FACT.

FACT.

After you have felt all the feelings, have a great big ugly cry and when you are done torturing yourself take a good look at the FACTS.

Facts will keep you honest.

Facts will keep you kind to yourself.

Facts will show you just how gnarly you can be at telling yourself stories and being a downright bully to yourself.

Feel it first than face the facts.

Winning combination every time.

Fact or Feeling,

you choose?

24.

INSIDE OUTSIDE, OUTSIDE INSIDE

If you have ever sought comfort, numbness, entertainment or solace in something to avoid feeling the way you're feeling, this is for you.

> Spoiler alert: We've all done it. I still do it occasionally. The issue is when it becomes a repeated pattern and it's not helping you live your life better. In fact, it's taking away from your quality of life and robbing you of experiencing a necessary part of yourself.

Searching outside of yourself to tend to an inside issue doesn't work long-term. Sure, a few drinks with a friend might be just what you need to destress from work but doing that every night would bring you undone. Sure, hitting a tub of ice-cream hard is a great way to enhance a movie experience. But constantly turning to food to take your mind off the hurt, trauma, break up, or shame, does nothing but delay the healing process. And more than likely get you up a few jeans sizes.

I completely understand why turning to drugs, alcohol, food, sex or whatever it is you numb out on works for a period of time. It works really well to stop you from feeling and thinking about what it is you're avoiding. Until, of course, when it doesn't. Then the repercussions of these behaviours catch up with you in other areas of your life and you are faced with the consequences of your choices and some really unhealthy coping mechanisms.

I, 100% numbed out for years with alcohol in my late teens to my late 20s. I couldn't be at a social event without a drink in my hand to curb the nerves. I would pre-game the pre-game drinks just to avoid feeling how I was feeling. And I woke morning after morning, weekend after weekend with a pit in my stomach over the blackout or recalling just how cringe worthy my behaviour was.

Sure, it worked for a while. Until it didn't.

> **Is there an area of your life where you prefer to numb out rather than deal with it?**
>
> **How's that working out for you?**

By the time he was born, I had hung up my party shoes for a solid four years, but hell hath no fury like years of unprocessed feels and really it was just a matter of time before I erupted all over the place. Even though I wasn't hitting the party scene, I was using other things to avoid feeling what I was feeling. I would work over it, exercise over it, socialise over it, and argued over it. Even though I was chugging green smoothies, meditating, doing yoga and hitting the farmers markets like an earth goddess, I hadn't yet done the emotional healing I had to do to free myself from a jail of my own making, so #nodeal.

The truth is, it's got to be dealt with. It's just got to.

By that I mean eventually you will have to face the limiting beliefs and bullshit stories you've been telling yourself and possibly forgive yourself for any mistakes you've made. That was a lot of my stuff. Mistakes. Guilt. Shame. Guilt being, I've done something bad. Shame being, I am bad. Mistakes were all the things that contributed to me feeling guilty and shameful. I had to face each one of these stories and work through them.

Asking myself questions like,

Is this really true?

What did you learn from this?

Does this actually make you a bad person?

Can you forgive yourself?

What can you do to love yourself more in this moment?

And then I would. I would even write letters of forgiveness to myself and process an entire scenario on paper, then light it up and release it to the universe. #Witchtalk I was so hellbent on releasing this one letter I was burning it on a super windy day. Just as it was turning to ash the wind got hold of it and blew it all over my deck. The very thing I was trying to get rid of surrounded me. My anxiety hit an all-time high. As I hosed and swept the embers up from my timber decking—remembering to check in shoes and under door mats—I was reminded I was being guided to really, *really* release that story. I had to work for that one or it literally would have burnt my house down.

Healing the inside comes through acknowledging the mess, then doing what you need to do to clean it up.

That's it.

Acknowledgement is owning your shit and destructive behaviours. Committing to creating new healthy habits and a life that's in alignment with the way you're wishing to move forward.

Simple. Messy.

A lifetime of commitment of checking in and choosing you.

The scariest part of all of this is taking the time to own it and see it for what it is. Once you are okay with doing that, you get the relief when you finally burn that bridge. Better the bridge than burning your entire house down, right?

Let the bridges we burn

light the way.

25.

GETTING ANXIOUS ABOUT GETTING ANXIOUS

I had an epiphany a while back; an epiphany I tell you, and it really shouldn't come as much of a surprise, because genius! I get anxious about getting anxious. I get anxious about getting anxious and as a result most of the OCD traits I have come about through a need to prevent worrying before it actually happens.

> **Any light bulbs here?**
>
> **Where in your life do you try to prevent anxiety from creeping up?**
>
> **Is there anything you do to avoid having to 'worry' about it later?**
>
> **Phone calls? Rituals? Daily tasks? Tapping something? Turning at the same point on your walk?**

Night times used to be a real crap storm for me emotionally. As soon as my head hit the pillow, I would worry about all sorts of mundane things, but I couldn't rationalise them to save my life. Before going to bed, I would have to check I turned the dryer off and all the taps. Why? Because these were the sorts of thoughts that would keep me up at night if I wouldn't go check on them. I remember I also had to make sure my wallet was there. I used to do this when I was younger too. When I was ten or eleven, I can't quite remember, my mum bought me a Macquarie Dictionary for school. It was $26, and that was a lot of money back then. I loved it and I was oh, so, grateful. I would always check to see that it was there before I left the house and again, that the power point to my keyboard was off.

Anxiety has been showing up for me most of my life.

Even up until just a few years ago, if I didn't consciously go around—so random—before bed, rest assured the overwhelm would take hold. I would be up checking to see if I turned the tap off, the dryer off, or that I'd locked my car. Sometimes, I would do it more than once and it wasn't actually ever about the taps or the dryer, I just didn't want to be worrying about the taps or the dryer. Don't even get me started on checking in on the boys before I'd go to bed. I still do that. I always watch to see if they're breathing. I always check Oakie's sleep sack for spiders before I put him in it, and I make sure there're no extra toys in his cot. If anything happened to the boys, I don't know what I would do, so I still have my little ways to ensure I minimise the worry and maximise their safety as I go to bed.

This is the thing with anxiety. When you experience a full-blown panic attack, as I did several times a day, for months, you try to do anything you can to avoid that.

You get anxious about getting anxious.

You also develop a whole heap of strategies you can do to help yourself feel better and possibly ward off an anxious spiral. The thing is though wizards, the more you try to control a spiral and avoid awakening the beast, the harder you make it for yourself. A need to control the future appears when you don't feel safe and anchored in your present.

Lightbulb, right?

For reals.

For me that turned out to be a massive change and a shit tonne of inner work, but you know, sometimes a new lip gloss or meditation might be the answer? Who knows? What I do know is this: Anxiety doesn't show up for *no* reason and there's always a deeper thread to it. Instead of running, avoiding it or being ashamed of it we can get a lot from unpacking it, embracing it and meeting it with compassion.

> The more we try to control and hold on, the harder it is to be in the flow.
>
> The more we fight the message, the harder it is to win the war.
>
> The more we worry about getting anxious, the more anxious we will be.

And so are the days of our lives

You don't feel things by accident, boo.

Edit your life often and see what gems are right under your nose.

Life is so beautifully messy and simply complicated.

The more we fight the message,
the harder it is to

win the war.

The more we worry about getting anxious,
the more anxious

we will

be.

26.

YOUR MESS WILL BE YOUR MAKING

Seriously, whoever started the memo we all have to have our shizzle together all the time deserves to be fired. I mean humaning is messy business. For real. There is not a day that goes by where I don't think I could have handled something better but I'm also okay with that because I'm learning.

I have had three conversations with three different women in the past twenty-four hours and each of them were shying away and slightly ashamed of their messy bits. Embarrassed by the struggles in their life, the pieces of themselves they wished they could sweep under the rug. The thing they don't realise is the pieces of themselves they are so ashamed of will be the parts of themselves that make them so flipping relatable to other women.

Your magic is in your mess.

That thyroid condition making losing weight challenging is actually the part of your story that will make your wellness journey so freaken inspiring and beneficial to be a part of.

The fear you have around dying is actually the ticket to show you how much you actually love your life. Your anxiety you're hiding from everyone will be the catalyst for your evolution and the start of so many, *holy shit, me too* moments that you can have between you and your friends.

Your mess is where the lessons are.

> **Throwback to some of your biggest uh-oh moments. Have you grown because of them?**
>
> **Think of your best friends, do you love them because they are perfect or because they are real, and you can be yourself around them?**

Your vulnerability is where your strength is and the things you are ashamed of are usually the very things that by owning, set you free.

For instance, I would not be me without anxiety. Even though, at this present moment in time, I can manage it and most days it sits happily in the back seat, but it will forever and always be a part of me and that is A-Okay. Why? Because it has to be and if you can't beat 'em, join 'em. One thing is for sure, we can change the stigma around anxiety and mental health. How? By showing the world that people just like you and I get anxious. That anxiety can and will look different for everybody and there's no shame in our game.

When I realised all those scary and overwhelming feels came under the umbrella of anxiety, I was relieved to know I wasn't crazy and these feels had a name. Not everyone in my circle felt that way. I've had people try to use it against me. I've had others believe it will hold me back. I've even had someone say I need to hide my anxiousness from my son so he doesn't catch it. I mean really, WTF? Anxiety doesn't mean you're broken; it just shows you care. A beautifully active mind can do so many amazing things and for us, this is just the beginning.

It's the same thing for whatever it is you feel you need to hide from the world. When you change the way you look at things, the thing you look at changes. So, when you change the way you view your 'mess' the way to handle it will ultimately shift. When you take your shadows out into the light, they don't look so scary anymore. We hold the key to our happiness and how our story will be written. All we have to do is decide which way we will move the pen.

Is there a part of yourself you can bring into the light? Next time a conversation arises where it's possible to keep it more on the real side, do you think you could try that? Instead of thinking *what will they think of me?* Can you try *what will make me feel good?* Let that be your compass.

> It's the parts where it all falls apart that can ultimately bring us all together.
>
> 'My mess will be my making.' Say that again for me.
>
> 'My mess will be my making.'

My mess will be

my making.

27.

DON'T WORRY

If you are in relationship and one of you is a little extra in the nervous or fearful feels, welcome to the gang. The only thing worse than watching someone you love experience anxiety is being the person who's caught in an anxious spiral. Please always remember that when you're about to blow a gasket. As frustrating, confusing and difficult as it is for you to wrap your head around, your partner is usually going through something much worse when it comes to moving through an anxiety attack.

> **The worst thing you can ever say to someone who is worried about something is 'just don't worry.' Have you ever said this to someone, or someone said this to you?**

Even though the way someone feels is completely out of your hands, when you love someone as much as I'm sure you do, you want to support them, right?

I've got you covered.

Here's a few things I've worked out to be true in the hopes that you can show up as the best 'thunder buddy' going around.

COMPASSION wins every time.
Attempt to understand. Provide reassurance and answer the same question fifty times if they need you to, without the huffs and puffs. Anxiety and a need to control or predict the future comes up when we don't feel safe and secure in our present. Use this knowledge to do whatever you can to make the moment safe again by engaging your partner in their *now*.

VALIDATE them.
Listen to them, empathise and show support. I know it can be frustrating and at times it may seem completely irrational to you. To your partner in that moment their feelings, thoughts and fears are as real as that coffee stain on your fresh white shirt right before a meeting. Completely jarring, totally uncalled for and a major inconvenience to them too.

BE THERE.
We don't need you to fix anything because we for sure aren't broken. What you may need to do is take the reins for a bit. Take the pressure off and be a loving force in the face of a war that no one can see. Make the decision for dinner or what to do today if that helps. Get out of the house for a change of scenery, take them with you of course, and be the voice of reason and loving acceptance.

CHANGE the CHANNEL.
Not on the TV because if your partner is losing their shit and you are still watching the TV, or your phone, then I'm guessing this may be a part of the problem. Bring up a new focus, change the outlook, shower them with love and remind them of what a great team you are. Sure, something might go wrong, but you'll face it together if it does.

>Things that will **_not_** help.

TOUGH LOVE.
This is the worst flipping idea. You can't discipline, force or scare anxiety out of someone. Making someone anxious about feeling anxious will give you front row seats to an unravelling of all sorts.

Telling someone to CALM DOWN.
No one in the world's history has ever calmed down by being told to calm down FFS. Just like no one who is feeling depressed has ever found their love of life again by being told to cheer up.

GETTING FRUSTRATED.
I know it's hard. I know it's repetitive but please know it's not about *you*. Whatever your partner is going through is a symptom of something else. It might be a limiting belief, an old story, a lack of self-worth. The best thing that you can do is to be there to support and encourage them while they figure out what that is and heal.

Anxiety is not an attribute of someone showing weakness, but a sign of someone who cares infinitely, who loves their life and wants to protect themselves and the people they love within it. You don't need to fix them because they aren't damaged. You don't need to change them because they are enough exactly as they are. What would be awesome is if you could stand next to them, love and encourage them to do the work so they can get to a place where they no longer fear their fears. Instead, they use them as stepping stone to a place of understanding who they are in a world that tells us all to be so many different things. Remind them often why you love them. Show them how much you care for them. If all else fails, laugh. Laughter will always make the harder parts of life a little easier. After all, you have each other, someone to care about and what could be more wonderful than that?

Anxiety is not an attribute
of someone showing weakness, but

a sign of someone who cares infinitely.

28.

IT'S THE TITS

I have always loved the saying 'it's the tits'. It's moderately offensive, sure, but it always, always, always makes me giggle. Usually because it's describing a particularly good type of food or drink in my circles, and perhaps because I have a sketchy sense of humour at best. It really is the tits.

Here's the thing though, this book is my attempt to make sense of that which doesn't and provide a little clarity on a few of the issues I see derail us. Our boobs or society's interpretation of them is one of them.

We are fed images all our lives of beautiful busty women with perfect hourglass figures and flawless perky breasts. They encourage us to believe they are the ultimate symbol that belong to all sexy and desirable woman. It comes through in cartoons, in magazines, in movies, porn and anywhere else women are portrayed. The thing is sex sells and I get that, but let's not get it twisted. Breasts are mounds of fat put on our chest to feed our infants. That's their job. Feeding our young. Whoever thought it was a red-hot idea to suggest, promote and sell the notion our boobs were meant to be perfectly symmetrical, perky and of ample size is a dick. I'd fully put my life savings on it he also has one.

> **Have you ever felt the pressure to have your breasts look a certain way?**
>
> **How did that make you feel?**

This topic has been at the forefront of my mind lately. I, too, fell into the trap of thinking a full rack would make me feel better about a lot of different things in my life. That bigger boobs would complete the me-package more. I listened to people when they made comments about others having great boobs and paid attention to what said boobs looked like. I was feeling quite lost, working overseas at that time and thought perhaps a boob job was the answer. After the surgery, my breastage was way bigger than what I had requested but I was too naïve to say anything and so I carried on. As I mentioned before, after nine-and-a-half-years one ruptured and they advised surgery ASAP.

I elected *not* to get them replaced.

I went through all the feels.

All of them. Relief. Regret. Anger. Fear. Sadness. Blame. Excitement. Seriously, a solid segway of emotions and a lot of soul searching. Here's the bullet point version.

- Breast Implants are made up of 30+ toxic chemicals we then choose to place incredibly close to our vital organs for years and years at a time.
- 50% of implants will either leak or rupture within a ten-year period.
- Slicing open my perfectly healthy pectoral muscle and the thousands of nerve endings within only to leave a plastic bag that will most likely lead to extra stress and pressure on my immune system doesn't seem like such a great idea after all.
- Bigger boobs just mean bigger bras.
- Your boobs are the most boring thing about you.

My goodness it was a ride. And as I sit here, drains at my side still collecting the oozing fluids coming out of the cavernous holes in my chest from the removal of these not-so-fun-bags, I am at peace.

I feel more me than ever before.

I am proud of my lopsided origami tits. I affectionately named them so because I believe I may have to fold them up to place them in a bra. I feel more confident already, even though I am wearing bags of fluid outside my body. I have nothing to hide behind anymore.

We choose the story.

We create the rules.

Our breasts are there for us and our bodies.

Our breasts will look how they look.

I will not say I love the look of my breasts, sisters, because I don't really. They look a little odd right now, but they are mine, all mine, and I've got nothing to feel self-conscious about.

May our breasts hang low and lopsided just as nature intended and may you always giggle when you hear someone say,

'It's the tits.'

Growing old is unavoidable if we're lucky but growing up is entirely optional.

My breasts.
My body.
My business.

29.
DO NO HARM, BUT TAKE NO SHIT

If you constantly find you're trying to prove your *Self* to someone, you have already forgotten your worth. This is something I have rubbed up against a lot in my trips around the sun, especially in the realm of relationships. Recently, I really liked a guy, nothing really happened, but I knew there were possibilities.

He did not.

I wasn't enough for him and whilst that's okay and I respect that, for a moment—read: a long time. I held onto this notion he would eventually see in me what I hoped and one day it would all come together.

It didn't.

We had mutual friends so often we would be thrown together, and I have a bucket full of funny yet embarrassing stories where I let him know how I felt. Some through jokes, some through texts and all of them putting myself out there. That's how I roll though, heart on sleeve, especially if there's been a celebratory cocktail in my hand. I must have really cared for him because the day I finally let this go it really hurt. It hurt for two big reasons.

1. Because I wasn't enough for him.
2. Because I didn't see how enough I was.

Fork it.

The real kicker was the second point. If I had realised how enough I was, then it wouldn't have bothered me he didn't believe that I was enough for him.

There is gold in these low points I tell ya.

I had a really low day. I mean *loooooow*. Heart on the floor, face in the dirt kinda low. This wasn't the first of those days around this situation, but this was a particular pearler where all I could do to move through it was acknowledge it and sleep it off. I didn't do anything extra on my dark day. I didn't show up any differently. I just had a case of the *sads* and let those I love know about it.

Sad days are okay.

Crying is important.

Broken hearts don't need to stay broken.

You know what else? Write this down: Sometimes we break our own hearts.

I did in this instance. Regardless of anything else or anybody else, I kept showing up to a closed door. Over and over again with hope in my heart and a future of dreams in my mind. The reality is my part in this is all mine and the only way to heal that is to change my story and validate and love on myself. FFS.

> **When was the last time you found yourself on the proverbial bathroom floor?**
>
> **How much did it hurt?**
>
> **Have you learnt anything from it?**

I know *for sure* I'm not the only gal out there who's done this.

At least, I think I'm not. Surely not? *Reader's note: Send help!* Joking.

If you find yourself in a story where you repeatedly are trying to hustle for your worthiness, leave. Whether you are actively and consciously pouring your heart out to someone or you notice you're doing it in silence, quit it. If you're forever going above and beyond at work doing anything for a scrap of praise yet repeatedly feeling undervalued, do something about it. Change what you're allowing it to mean to you and about you or address it. If you know in your heart of hearts the way you're showing up to face something within your life isn't aligned with your best self and nourishing you from the inside out, I say this. For forks sake, woman, get your shizzle together and acknowledge your worth.

Know your worth, sista, and then add tax.

Examine what you tolerate.

Examine the stories around your sense of self.

Remind yourself daily in any situation where you feel less than.

Repeat for life.

Examine what you *tolerate.*

30.

STOP SAYING YES TO SHIT YOU HATE

For real, why do people still do that? I can get all judgy on you here because you will rarely, if ever, see me doing something I hate. Let me talk you through it. Have you found yourself saying 'yes,' because you want them to like you, or you fear disappointing someone, or worried they won't love you unless you 'do the thing'? Do you really think that's a fair foundation to build a relationship on or to nurture a relationship with someone on these grounds? Hell to the no, lady friend.

The second you say yes to something that doesn't align with how you feel or what you know is best for your mind, body and spirit, it's like you flip your soul the bird, and maybe even spit. Seriously, though, I know that's a solid comment, but the visual is worth the shock value.

I'll say it again.

Every time you say yes to something that doesn't align with you; you're giving your soul the rude finger. Every decision we make either moves us towards alignment or out of it.

Towards love or away from it.

Saying yes to shit you hate, is saying someone else's needs are more important than your own. That someone's desires are more important than your own, and what you want doesn't matter.

What a beat down.

Get back in your box hopes and dreams, there's no place for you here.

Am I overreacting? Absolutely not.

> **Can you see the areas of your life where you have slipped or are slipping into people pleasing mode?**
>
> **How's that feeling for you?**

Even on a cellular level we are vibrating alongside the choices we make. We are communicating with the universe at every step and co-creating with every breath. It's how we roll. If you are putting it out there to the universe that your dream doesn't matter and it's okay for you to take a back seat, someone will miss out on a lollypop the day they're handed out. It's not okay to break a promise to yourself. Every time you do that you are creating a precedent to allow it to happen again. If you say *yes* to something that should have been a *no*, I'm 93.7% sure you will resent them for it. Even more so if the desired effect was to get recognition or acknowledgement for doing the thing and you didn't get it. We've all been there for sure, but this one is on us. If you say yes to something with the expectation it would get you love, acknowledgement, recognition or about ten other things like that, you will be disappointed and it's time to look at your intentions and motives for saying yes. If it's pure and from the goodness of your heart, rock on sista. You go, Glen Coco! If, however, you're doing it for something in return then I suggest you put the doughnut down and back away from the table.

How do you get around feeling resentful and harbouring a diary filled with obligations to things and events that are sucking the life from your soul?

You slow down your *yes*.

Slow it all the way down and ask yourself, 'What am I really feeling here? If I say, *Yes*, to this, what am I saying *No* to?' That will tell you there and then if it's worth the trade off and if it will lift you up and raise your spirits or if it will kick your soul in the vag.

If you struggle with saying no, I think you will love the next chapter.

If it's not a 'Hell Yes', it's a *'Fuck No'*.

31.
'NO' IS A COMPLETE SENTENCE

Do you feel you need to justify or explain yourself to others? I thought so. I'm going to keep it really simple to start with.

YOU DON'T.

Not even a little bit.

> A reminder in the words of Glennon Doyle: "The most revolutionary thing a woman can do is not ask permission—and then not explain herself."

At any given moment you have the answers to everything you seek inside you. I'm not sure where or why it started but somewhere around the traps women started to doubt their ability to know what's best for them. On top of that they then felt the need to justify their choices, just in case someone might perceive them to be anything other than agreeable. So, this has probably been hundreds, if not thousands of years of programming, but, friend, those days are gone. You don't need to run anything by anyone. You don't need to seek out your friend to see what they think first. It's not essential to get three people to deliberate or say yes and offer up a field of yellow daisies before deciding. Only you know what's right for you.

> **The question is, what's it going to take to learn to trust yourself?**
>
> **How can you take steps towards validating yourself and being your own cheerleader?**
>
> **Why are you seeking approval outside of yourself?**

Most of the reasons I can come up with while I sit here in my Ugg boots is that it all stems back to feeling fear and that you are not enough.

Fear of being judged.

Fear of getting it wrong.

Fear of upsetting people.

It has to be right? Why? Because under all of that, you don't believe in your enough-ness. What I know for sure is that you are enough. You already are. You were born a leader of this body of yours. While it's fun to share your path with others and talk about life and all the things that come with it, the decisions on what you do in that time only needs to come from you. With that, you also don't need to validate your decision to anyone. If they ask and you want to share, go for it. If they ask and you don't feel you want to share a super mature response, I like to roll with this:

'Because, I want to.' 'Because you want to' is the best dang reason for anything I think. There are more eloquent ways to put it, of course.

'I felt like this was the best option for me.'

'After weighing everything up, I've concluded this decision will impact my life, and everyone I'm involved with by association in the most positive light.'

Or, 'Because I said so.'

Still a fave.

You can say no and not explain yourself if it doesn't align with you.

You can say no, thank you, if you want to be polite about it. Which I do because there's no need to be rude, really.

You can say 'thank you so much for the offer, but that doesn't feel right for me, so, no,' and leave it at that if you want. The flip side of this is saying yes to whatever and whoever you want. That, of course, is entirely up to you.

You don't need to ask permission.

You don't need to pull an oracle card.

You don't need to wait for the planets to align.

You don't need to set an intention.

You don't need to wait for a sign or diffuse your oils before saying yes.

You know what's right for you by the way it feels.

The truth and your next right move will feel expansive and full of possibility. Your heart may open, it will feel light and true. How do you get there? You feel into it. Play out both scenarios in your mind. Whichever direction feels like the right one for you, trust it. We always know the next right step, but first we have to get out of our own way to experience it.

'No',

is a complete sentence.

32.

HOLD YOUR GAZE

I was listening to a podcast the other day, and it centred around human connection and the ways we *do* or *don't* do it. What it highlighted for me was that so often we look away right at the moment when we could be leaning in.

Here's the context that made me be all like, *Oooooooh, okay, I get it.* There's a guy my friends and I think is very nice. I see him occasionally around the place and we can refer to him as Hot Josh. This isn't his name, obvs. But for the purpose of his anonymity and this story, we'll change his name. Anyway, we have bumped into each other a few times and the chat has always been very profesh but every time he made eye contact, I couldn't hold it because; cue, all the feels. You know the ones where you get that rush, or uncomfortableness? There's like a heat, it's intense. That's what it is, yes, it's an intensity, and it's bloody unnerving. The thing is, if I looked away every time he looked at me, how would he ever know I was interested? If I couldn't hold my gaze, how could I possibly hold anything else together? What signals were I giving Hot Josh if I blew off every moment of connection?

I tell you what I was doing, and I demonstrated that:

a) I'm so unsure of myself.

b) He's not worthy of my attention.

c) The floor is way more interesting.

Cue the light bulb moment. Holy shirt.

The messages I was sending out to him were the polar opposite of what I wanted them to be. I was interested, but I was avoiding that intensity because it made me uncomfortable. It turns out what I want in a relationship and in my life is that exact intensity and curiosity I had been avoiding and I think I've been doing it my entire life!

FFS.

How's your eye contact game?

Are you a soulful gazer or an avert your eyes gal at heart?

How do you feel in situations where eye contact is needed?

At work? With your family? In interviews?
At school with other parents?

How do you feel when having a conversation?
Where do you look?

What I want in life in terms of a romantic relationship is a partnership where we choose each other every day. What I was demonstrating here is that I couldn't even hold my shirt together long enough to connect eye to eye so I was sabotaging any chance of a connection before we could even see if there was one. To put you out of suspense, nothing happened with Hot Josh, but once I realised this, the next time I bumped into him I looked him in the eye. We had proper conversations. Wouldn't you know it, he shared more about his life with me. I understood a little more about him. I showed up, and I took my body with me. And even though it was so uncomfortable for me to present in that intensity, what's the alternative, a constant disconnection? Yeah, nah, no thanks. The disconnect was in me knowing my worth and allowing my body to be in that.

Tara Bliss speaks of this with her 'take your body with you' chats. We do so much work on up-levelling our self-worth, our mindset and our businesses, but what about our body? We have to take these vessels with us. We have to get into our body, move our body, connect with our body and feel into all the feelings we experience. I thought my self-love and respect game was strong, but there was a kink. While I thought I was ready to *be* in the moment and have these moments within my life, by looking away and shying away from intense or big feels I was telling my body I wasn't worthy, that this was wrong or I'm undeserving. That's not true. The first step to changing the game was acknowledging I had a kink in the first place. BOOYAH!

> Update: Now I hold the vision of others as long as possible without it becoming creepy.

I realised this applies to so much more than romantic or potential partners. This is a *life* thing. So many of the things we want in this lifetime will make us uncomfortable. So many of the things we desire will test us, to have us feeling the full spectrum of intensity and passion but if we turn our gaze away from everything that brings up intense emotions or physical reactions, where will that leave us? Up shirt creek without a paddle. Never knowing what could be and always feeling like you're missing out on something and essentially robbing yourself of the very thing that you desire most. Yuck.

    What to do now? Now, we connect.

Now, we learn to get comfortable with the uncomfortable; we take our body along for the ride. We don't shy away from the big expansive and intense feels if it brings us closer to what we want. We know our worth and we don't step away from people.

    We hold our gaze.

    We hold our gaze.

We look, but

how often do we actually see?

33.

YOU'RE HEARING, BUT ARE YOU LISTENING?

Who has been in a conversation with someone when they say something that triggers you? For the rest of the chat you can't focus on anything else but the few words that sparked your interest or anger. And now you're off in your own world quite possibly missing the context of what your friend is trying to convey. Dude. I get it. But how much of what you heard was actually true and not just your interpretation of what you thought they were trying to say? Listening to someone is a full body thing. It's not just about what we *hear*, it's also about what we *feel* with our body, what we *see*, how they move their eyes—expressions—how they fidget and how they are conveying their words to you. The body doesn't lie and sometimes the most important part of what someone says actually doesn't use any words.

I'm a good listener. I know this, but I also know I could be better, and this is something I'm working on in the realms of personal development. I'm the first to put my hand up and say I used to and sometimes still do bring a conversation back to my experiences when it's time to share. Is this wrong? I'm not sure but I'm super conscious of letting others have their moment and doing my very best to listen. Not only with my ears but also with my eyes and heart. I have almost stopped giving advice entirely because unless someone asks for it directly, that's not usually what they need. When someone comes to you and needs to offload, they generally aren't looking for a fix or for a solution. They have everything they need themselves to get from A to B, but what they need is someone to listen, to hold space and nod when appropriate or get angry in support of them when called for. Not everyone is ready for practical encouragement. Sometimes we just need a rant. The thing is though, if we see someone hurting, being the compassionate and caring people that we are, naturally we want to help them. This of course is robbing our friend of some purely cathartic ratchet talk where the opportunity to get it off their chest is what they need more than anything.

> **Are you ready to simply listen more?**
>
> **Do you feel that could be of benefit to those you love and engage with?**

The best thing you can do is sit down, lean in and listen.

Listen to what they are actually saying.

Let them have their moment.

Hold off telling her she should dump in, quit her job or get a fringe unless you're asked directly.

It's OKAY for me to

BE here.

34.

YOU COMPLETE ME

Woah. Woah. Woah. WOAH.

I take a teeny tiny issue with this. Most people would say this, or allude to this often, without ever really stopping to think what it is they're actually saying. Phrases like, my better half or, you complete me, imply you are walking around as half a person. Think about it for a minute. If you're cruising around longing to find your match so at long last you may feel whole, that's a lot of pressure you're unknowingly putting on someone else. Seriously. What may seem like a romantic gesture leaves someone you want to care about solely responsible for your happiness. What a load.

    Anytime you're *not* happy, it becomes their fault.

    Anytime you're sad, it's their responsibility to lift you up.

    Anytime you're *not* feeling loved, you're making it their job to be the one who dives in and lifts you out of the slump.

Woah.

What if, instead of looking for your other half, you came to the relationship whole? You take responsibility for your own happiness.

If you are sad, you find ways to move through it.

If you aren't feeling loved, you do whatever you need to fill your own cup up so you're never completely dependent on someone else again to sit in the warm and fuzzies.

> **How do you feel about this idea?**
> **Empowered? Mad? Hopeful?**

When you meet someone who you love doing life with, who is part of so many of your favourite moments and shares all the highs and the lows with you, you choose them. They choose you. Neither of you put the pressure on each other to be anything more than what you already are, then you can just enjoy each other.

Sign me up for that!

Which out of the two relationship styles would be more enjoyable to be a part of and which one do you think would last longer? For reals right. I for sure have been in the first one, many times over, but I feel like I have broken this pattern now. Finally. No, there's no fella on the scene but I have taken time to learn about what I need. And as equally important, what I can bring to a relationship when I show up as my whole self. A big thing going forward will be to watch the narrative in my mind around what it's meant to be and how it's meant to look. Being open to it looking a zillion different ways opens you up to magic you may have never even known you wanted until it appeared. Getting clear on how you want to feel within a relationship has huge weight to it too. Feeling the way you want to feel is a more accurate barometer of how good a pairing is for you for the space that you're in. Getting clear on what you want and how you want to feel doesn't mean you *need* to put together a list of how you want to feel but it's a great idea to do so. If you don't, the universe will keep serving you up something similar but not quite right. You'll confuse *right* with *familiar* and there's a massive difference in how both will play out.

I know there are plenty of people out there who look for 'the one', or your 'perfect match'. I don't believe there is a textbook perfect match for anyone. There are people we love, enjoy and who are worth the effort and work it takes to commit to co-creating a beautiful and lasting relationship. There are people our hearts recognise, feel great with and add so much happiness to our lives, but you could have many of those in your life. A soul mate doesn't need to be your lover, they can be your best friend or a sister. Your soul can find itself linked to another for many reasons, and according to Carolyn Myss, our souls have contracts with many, many people, throughout our lives.

True love can take many forms. Soul mates can be for a reason, a season or a lifetime. The one is the one you choose, but that can depend on who you are and what you're facing at the time. Expecting someone to be your everything is too much for one person to bare. Don't put that pressure on each other's hearts, that's a weight that can become too much to carry. The love of your life is real. The loves of your life are invaluable and important and every relationship you inevitably find yourself in is there to teach us about the world or ourselves.

There are so many ways to find and be love in this human form, but I know with absolute certainty the only one who can help you to feel whole and complete is *you*.

I am

whole.

35.

SHOULD-ING ALL OVER YOURSELF

Human-ing is a messy gig. There's no instruction manual or rule book or anything that even resembles something like that. All we have is our intuition as an internal compass but to get to that you've got to stop your mind from taking over. Quite the dance let me tell you.

Both the boys are with their dad for the day and I've felt so unsure what to do with myself. I've felt like I should make today super productive and also felt like I just want to lay on the couch and hide. I've wanted to work on my book but felt like I should also be outside. I've wanted to fit in all my appointments while I don't have the cubs because I should, but also not waste my day attending appointments. I was in a state of low-level panic and angry at myself for not utilising my free time to the best of my ability. Seriously?

So, as I do, because y'all know I love me some self-inquiry and this elephant on my chest is no stranger to me, I asked myself some questions.

What is this feeling that's coming up for me?

What am I letting this story mean for me?

How do I want to proceed?

Here's my answers sweet pea.

I'm scared, anxious and unsure.

I don't want to do the wrong thing and waste this time I have to myself.

Why? Because I really need it, and I don't want to feel like I screwed it up.

Why? Because I don't like feeling that I wasted a moment or made a mistake.

Compassion. I give myself permission not to fill the silence. I give myself permission not to fill the gaps. I give myself permission not to feel guilty.

> **When was the last time you felt the pressure to be or do things a certain way?**
>
> **You didn't want to waste your time?**
>
> **You didn't want to sleep away your holiday?**
>
> **You can't rest because there's housework to do, work to be done, emails to answer?**

It's been a while since I've felt this way, but I realise I've been pulling this crap when I don't have plans locked in for as long as I can remember. I know how precious time is. I also know how paralysing anxiety is and I don't want to spend any of my life moments feeling like they should be more. Isn't that what it really comes down to? When we start should-ing all over ourselves, we're basically slamming the door on the universe like an ungrateful teenager saying that this moment isn't enough, and we want more.

So rude of us btw.

There's also the deeper level here that's a real eye opener. Perhaps the reason we guilt trip over the moment we're in is because we don't feel worthy enough to just be as we are.

Fork.

I didn't even see that one coming. I just got out of the shower and felt inspired to tickle the keys and the realisation hit me like your first swing at a piñata. Savage and a little awkward.

Where did the pressure come from to make every moment count? Is it the 'Magic Happens' or the 'Make Every moment Count' bumper stickers getting around? Making every moment count adds a lot of pressure to our lives in general. Every moment counts, but the fact we're breathing is enough. Life isn't like one of those adult colouring books we all have somewhere. We don't have to colour in every space and we for sure don't have to stay between the lines. It's okay to leave some room to breathe, and it's okay to go rogue and see what comes up for you. I make stick figures look fat, so I appreciate a solid guideline and to worship someone else's art, but let's not lose our freedom to go our own way in the midst of our *during*.

THE TAKE AWAY

Permission not to fill the gaps.

Permission to let it look how it looks.

You are enough and the moment you're in is perfect as it is.

GAME. CHANGER.

Wouldn't you know it with this realisation and a moment to pause I came back to my breath, my body softened, and the words and lightness came with it? We don't need to fill up every second of life for it to be valuable. We don't need feel guilty for having space within our day. We certainly don't need to seek outside of ourselves for permission and it really helps if we are open to how it's going to look.

That's the key.

Be open to letting it look anyway at all, as long as it feels good for you.

Let it be

simple.

36.

SILENCE IS THE BEST SOUND

I'm sensitive to noise. If there's a lot of it and I'm trying to think I'm like a pressure cooker. Or maybe I'm like a time bomb, or a grenade, either ways it's dicey.

One of my boys is incredibly vocal. There's not a moment of silence throughout the day. From the second he wakes, until his head hits the pillow, he's singing, acting, fighting, asking questions, more questions, arguing, challenging, negotiating and also loving on me. I know he's a bright kid, but my challenge within it all is that I need silent pockets within my day.

    I love quiet.

    I mean I really, really love it.

    If I could I would marry it.

    I love quiet time.

In fact, I need it and we really all need it.

These days we are always on. We are spoilt for choice at what we can listen to at any given moment. We have podcasts, ted talks, radio, music and then there's everything we can watch: Netflix, Stan, Foxtel, 24/7 TV shows, You Tube, Insta Stories. It's endless. Add to that the sounds of our daily lives and it's no wonder that for many of us, unless you consciously seek it out, you won't be in silence very often.

When I was at my most anxious I used to avoid the silence because then I would have to think. Perish the thought. I would always make sure I had music or a guided meditation or a chakra cleanse or something to fill the silence. Always. At home I did course after course. I never allowed myself to sit still because of what would come up for me.

What would come up, I hear you ask? Oh, just everything I have ever done that I'm not proud of. Like when I said the wrong thing. I drank too much or hurt someone with my words—all of it—I would replay it over and over and attempt to distract myself from it, so I didn't have to feel it. I had lived my life as a master distracter. Able to switch gears in the blink of an eye. Until I couldn't anymore after the birth of my first son and all those worries and shame points bubbled to the surface. This is what has to happen though if we want to be free of them.

> **How comfortable are you with your thoughts?**
> **Do you welcome them or run from them?**

I was in a session with a client this morning and I realised I'm not sure I've ever verbalised how to shift and sort through those feelings before. I know you would have heard me speak about feeling it to heal it, but what does that even look like? And why on earth would you want to unleash that Pandora's box of emotions upon yourself.

I totally get it.

Here's the thing though, they don't all come up at once. You'll be going about your business and something will come to mind. A shame point for instance and normally your instinct will be to run and avoid. Instead, I want you to feel it and become a student of your emotions.

> What am I feeling right now?
>
> Why is this memory coming up for me?
>
> What did I learn about myself from this experience?
>
> How can I see this with compassion?

And I know once you see the gift in the answers, and you forgive yourself for being human or not knowing what you didn't know, you will soften, and *it* can move through. Will this same memory come back? Maybe, most probably, but you just repeat the process again. And it will be a little quicker this time because you know how to forgive yourself or others and how to get to a compassionate place quicker. Eventually that thought won't bother you and that's how you move through. That's how you heal. That's how you choose to see things differently by getting still and embracing the silence to allow you to hear the undercurrents of your mind's tides.

Pretty effing spectacular really.

On a scientific level you're creating new neural pathways.

On a spiritual level you're releasing things that were never yours to carry.

On an emotional level you're choosing forgiveness and compassion over everything and that gift is often found in *silence*.

One of my favourite *sounds* ever.

You don't need to fill

the silence.

37.

HURT PEOPLE, HURT PEOPLE

Today I was on the receiving end of a gnarly email. It was mean, uncalled for and incredibly hurtful and to say it didn't affect me would be an outright lie. It cut me deeply. Upon reading it, the words felt like they'd punched me in the stomach. It sucked the wind from me; the tears welled up and immediately I reached out to my friend for some support. Even knowing what I know about people who set out to tear others down, it still feels really good to talk it through with a friend you can trust. As women, I think that's how we do some of our very best processing—through a good rant.

> **How do you handle it when people lash out at you?**
> **Do you find that you respond or react?**

Here's what I know for sure now the initial disbelief has worn off. This is where I've landed.

Hurt people, hurt people.

Glennon Doyle explains this so perfectly. "Pain is not a hot potato to pass on to the next person or generation. And pain is not a mistake to fix. Pain is just a sign a lesson is coming. Discomfort is purposeful: it is there to teach you what you need to know so you can become who you were meant to be. Pain is just a travelling professor. When pain knocks on the door—wise ones breathe deep and say: 'Come in. Sit down with me. And don't leave until you've taught me what I need to know.'"

Not everyone is ready to learn from their pain and not everyone is ready to face what's in front of them. For many people it's easier to lash out at someone else and take their fury at the situation out on them. Instead of facing the truth they try to pass their pain on like a hot potato to someone else. Instead of taking responsibility they look to blame someone else. And instead of looking to reflect and heal they look to attack someone else. What can we do about the people and instances lumped on us? Feel what we need to feel and then when you're ready, see it compassionately.

I know you'll want to retaliate.

I know that you'll want to defend yourself.

I know that you'll want to have your say, make your peace, clear your name.

Is it going to change their beliefs?

Probably not.

Is it going to make them see how wrong they are?

I doubt it very much.

Is it going to be an act of passing the hot potato back to them?

100%.

Some people fight fire with fire, but in my experience, everybody gets burned. Today I am choosing to rise from the ashes and deal with it the only way I know how. Through words. Through processing. Through attempting to understand someone else's pain. I will be damn sure I'm not taking it on as my own though. This is not a perfect recipe for 'woke-ness' as I know from firsthand even as a sensitive soul we can only take so much before we are all like *woah, woah, woah, woah. Back the bus up* and we have to defend ourselves.

I get that.

I'm sure there's people out there to attest to the fact I can only take so much and if you keep poking the bear, eventually I'll roar. It's not about being 100% non-reactive. It's about bringing consciousness to the equation and choosing the response that feels right to you and where you are in your growth.

Hurt people, hurt people.

Does it make it sting any less?

No.

Does this realisation help you heal and move through your feelings with less collateral damage?

Absolutely.

Hurt people, hurt

people.

38.
WHO DOES SHE THINK SHE IS?

*"Who does she think she is?
It appears she is someone who is living her life,
unconcerned with whom you think she is."*
Brendon Burchard

It's taken me thirty-something years and many kicks in the proverbial teeth to get to the realisation of what other people think of you is none of your business. Why? Because it doesn't matter.

> What's your relationship with other people's opinions?
>
> How do the effect you within your life?
>
> Have they stopped you from moving forward with something you love?
>
> Have you censored yourself around other people? Imagine if you didn't?

I have spent too long in this lifetime worrying about what people will say, fixating on ways to make things right. Hoping if I say this, or do that, *they* will understand where I'm coming from. They will never understand because some people don't want to.

This is okay.

Give it a minute to sink in, but it will be okay.

When you quit doing things for the approval of others and you ask your heart the questions, everything shifts. Now, I'm not suggesting you forego your round table chats with your best girls where you rant about all the things. I'm not suggesting you don't call your mum or closest lady friend to blow off a little steam and share some news. I'm certainly not telling you to close off your ears to all advice. What I am telling you is to trust yourself enough to answer the question.

I will walk you through a cosmically magic friend of mine. Honestly, her energy is all glittery and light. Let's call her Hailey. Hailey has the most beautiful philosophies on living naturally and sustainably. She walks the walk and talks the talk and it's a beautiful way to be.

With the birth of her second baby approaching, all the fears started coming up for her. She had always wanted to birth at home. She had created such a strong story about what this would mean for her and her mothering journey, but it was causing a huge amount of anxiety. The birth of her first beautiful babe started at home but ended in hospital thanks to a few complications. This was the best outcome for all involved but the story of what birthing at home meant to her remained. Hailey was going around in circles looking for guidance from a variety of sources until we sat down together. You see, the anxiety was coming up because she was missing the message. Anxiety doesn't appear when we are in tune with our own intuition, it comes when we try to override or tune it out. Once Hailey got out of her head and back into her body, the answers became obvious. When she asked herself a few simple questions like, what is the ultimate outcome for this birth and where will make me feel most comfortable given my experiences for that to happen?

She had her answer.

One path flooded her body with anxiety and the other didn't.

Of course, there were people who would try to sway her decision but when Hailey came back to her *why*, their opinions became irrelevant.

The answer she chose isn't important, but the person she trusted to make the final call is everything—*herself*.

I am my own

answer.

39.
ALL'S FAIR IN LOVE AND WAR

Pfft, what a forking joke.

Nope, not all's fair in love and war. I call BS on this one.

NEXT!

Just kidding. No really. Relationships are complicated things. I have learned more about relationships in the past couple of years whilst not being in one than what I'd ever thought possible. So much of that learning has come through Christal Fuentes aka The Ladies Coach, and her podcast. I just knew I had to sit her down and ask her to give me her spin on this simply complicated element of love.

The first thing I asked Christal straight out of the gate was, "Do you think all's fair in love and war? And what's your immediate reaction to that phrase?"

"The first thing I'd say is . . . 'what *dude* said this?'" She continued.

"I'd be right because only a *dude* would compare love to war. But before I get into my thoughts about this phrase, let's get a little backstory of where it comes from. The exact quote is *"the rules of fair play do not apply in love and war,"* and comes from a play written by John Lyly called *Euphues*. Now, I'm not a literary genius by any stretch of the imagination but when we dissect the context in which this quote was written, Lyly was using it to describe the flaws of humanity and how humans can become desperate to serve their own needs, especially in emotional situations.

As a relationship coach, I can definitely agree that intimate love can shine a light on the internal battles and wounds within us. Our internal wounds are what we ultimately project onto others, which completely damages the sanctity of relationships. And our wounds as a society are what continue to cause destruction around us.

Do I believe this quote to be a justification for the pain people either accept or project onto relationships? HELL NO! Just because this is "human nature" doesn't mean we should accept this as a standard.

Another thing I would expand on here is if we look closely at works of literature, mythology, and patterns of history, we will see that we have been WARNED about what toxic masculinity can and will do.

"All's fair in love and war," is a belief that lacks feminine core values. It suggests that it is okay to be disruptive as long as you get what you want. Unfortunately, we see this still play out in society or our own personal relationships."

I'm not a huge fan of love being compared to a battlefield because that's playing up to the idea we should be on separate sides. As a relationship coach I know Christal works with couples on the reg, so I asked what she would say to people who feel like they're no longer on the same team?

> "If you feel like you and your partner aren't on the same team, it usually means trust has been compromised. That doesn't necessarily mean betrayal. It means both of you have failed to validate, acknowledge and affirm each other's needs. When one or both people don't feel seen, heard and understood in a relationship, that is where the breakdown happens. You will feel alone and when you feel alone you no longer feel safe in the relationship.
>
> So, what do you do? You start to defend yourself from the other person because you feel they no longer have your best interests at heart. You unconsciously play in different teams without knowing you are, and as long as you are on different teams and emotions are heightened, well... "All's fair in love and war," right?
>
> P.S. This breakdown not only happens in personal/intimate relationships, but this is also happening with world leaders. But I digress.
>
> Here are some things I suggest you look at when you feel disconnected from your partner and don't know what to do:
>
> 1. What are you ultimately crying out for? Ask yourself this simple question: What do I wish they'd validate,

acknowledge and or, affirm in me? Like I said before, we are all just trying to be seen, and if we don't feel seen we will act out in ways our higher selves would not be proud of.

2. What is my partner trying to communicate that I'm not hearing and instead, dismissing?

3. Could my partner's request be triggering my deepest fear? There might be a part of us that's rejecting our partner's needs because it triggers a fear within.

4. What would happen if you caved in? You know the saying, "pick and choose your battles," but what would happen if you dropped the rope and stopped playing tug 'o' war with your partner and let go of the resisting? Would it expand the relationship or compromise who you are?

Most of the time, we are in resistance mode for no reason because of this humanly desire to be right. Which goes back to what, I think, John Lyly was trying to portray in his play."

I seriously love this woman.

We all know and have heard a bazillion times relationships aren't easy. We get that. But sometimes we put up with way too much because we think it's just meant to be hard right? It's that—all's fair in love and war—all relationships are meant to be work vibe. Christal and I have been friends for a while and she shares this often in her podcast, so I know she *knows* they also shouldn't be all work. I asked Christal to run us through that and here is what she said,

"Let's get real for a second. You are not here for your relationship. I love my man, but I was not birthed onto this Earth for him, and likewise. We have our own purpose, mission and desires.

Your relationships should amplify your mission not BE the mission. When we stay struggling in relationships it makes our lives about another person. Which not only restricts you but also puts a whole lot of expectation and pressure on your significant other.

I definitely am a firm believer that a relationship—all relationships around us—is what makes the soul evolve and that struggle is actually necessary, but I think it's also important to remember, you are here for your OWN JOURNEY.

Not for anyone else, which is why the term "soul mate" and "the one" irritates me because when you give people significant labels it potentially:

1. Keeps you in unhealthy relationships longer than need be because they are your "soul mate," and if they are your "soul mate" this is what the universe must want you to go through, right?
2. Put's too much pressure on your partner. It puts your happiness in their hands and that's an unrealistic responsibility for anyone to take on.
3. When they show their "human side" flaws, insecurity, emotion and pain, we don't know how to handle it and get fearful.

Sure, relationships take work, but how much work until

it takes away from the essence of who you are? And is the work you are doing in your relationship catering to a unified vision or just a distraction?

Everyone is responsible for mastering themselves, are you with a partner who will learn from mistakes and have the capacity to do the work with you? Or are you rowing this boat alone?

Going back to playing on the same team. When you think about a team, everyone on the team has their own roles that cater to a unified vision. How can both of you bring the WHOLE YOU to the table to cater to this relationship? When both people show up fully, you won't stay in the struggle mode of your relationship very long."

Now, if that doesn't get your brain ticking over then I'm a monkey's uncle. We have all been in relationships at some point where elements of this is the case. Understanding why that's come about and how to heal from it and move forward is key and no one explains it as well as Christal Fuentes aka The Ladies Coach.

If you're not on

the same team,

you're in the wrong game.

40.

SOMETIMES SAYING NOTHING, SAYS THE MOST

One of the biggest growth opportunities I've had in the last couple of years is that I don't have to attend every argument I'm invited to. And in that, it means I don't always have to defend myself. There is a real art to not engaging. I used to be an incredibly reactive person and can see now that so much of it was coming from a lack of belief in myself so if I was ever challenged, I fought back. I didn't have a strong enough belief system, so I spent way too much time fighting to prove my point and trying to convince others of my validity. Someone who's fighting to prove their point sounds like someone who's strong within themselves, I guess; however, someone who is so strong on their way and secure in themselves doesn't feel the need to stop and throw stones at every dog that barks. They just go about their day.

Lightbulb! Winner!

This changed everything for me.

We don't need everyone to believe and carry our point of view. It's not our job to convince and convert everyone to our way of life. It's not our way or the highway. If someone thinks you're a dick, do you think giving them a list of all the reasons you're not a dick will make them think you're any less of one? I have been on the receiving end of some gnarly growth opportunities in my time. Like next level hate being slung at me. It takes everything I have in my tank not to fight back and explain myself. It's taken willpower and a strength of spirit I didn't know I had to be all like, *whatever, I know it's not true*. And it has taken many tears; a butt load of self-reflection and wheelbarrow loads of inner work to get to a place where I can see that the best thing that I can do in a situation is to say *nothing*.

Sometimes saying nothing says the most.

> **How does standing strong in your worth make you feel?**
>
> **Have you needed to retaliate more than you'd like?**
>
> **Do you move past feelings easily or do you stay stuck marinading over them for days?**

When we say nothing, we are ultimately saying you aren't even going to give whatever *that* was any airtime. It's saying you are solid enough in who you are to not feel you have to rationalise another's word vomit. By saying nothing it shows you have way more important things to do than deal with whatever poo-pie was just served up.

Is it easy to do that?

Fork no.

Is it worth it to do that?

Hell yes.

If you're still not convinced reread chapter 37: Hurt People, Hurt People. The anger someone flashes out at you generally has nothing to do with you and everything to do with them. My final point on this is, do you think responding to whatever *that* is will make a difference?

Highly unlikely.

So, if you find yourself in a situation where you've been here before, you know your words will go in one ear and out the other and frankly there's no point in retaliating.

Don't engage.

Please, don't engage.

It doesn't condone the behaviour. And it doesn't mean you're a pushover or gutless. It means you're saving your energy for more magical endeavours. How can you be heard though, and how can you show true conviction and depth of your character?

Live it.

Live it in every way, in every day.

Show the world your passions by living and working for them.

The best way to change the world is to start by changing your own. The best way to help the world heal is to start by healing yourself and let that be a light that inspires others.

The best way to show you walk your talk, speak your truth and are who you say you are is to stop wasting your time trying to prove it. Instead, spend your time embodying it.

You won't change the world by trying to prove you can. You'll change the world by being the person who does.

41.

BOUNDARIES ARE NOT FENCES

If you've ever felt taken advantage of, walked over, not seen, or not validated, then there's a really high chance they've encroached your boundaries and blurred the lines. This *feeling* is your signal. You're not feeling the way you want to feel because there's an area of your life where you're doing too much, not doing enough or someone is doing something that no longer resonates with you. Basically, someone or something has crossed a boundary, but more often than not we haven't implemented them yet. This feeling of being pissed, over worked or undervalued is your first signal of where it might be a good idea to look at creating a loving boundary.

> **Where are the areas of your life that could benefit from a loving boundary, or seven?**

So, my beautiful friend, I hear you ask, 'what is a boundary?' Great question, you're great at this.

A boundary is your bottom line.

A boundary is the guiding rules for your life.

A boundary outlines what you will tolerate.

It helps you keep things in and also manages things by keeping them at a safe distance. Think of them as your self-care support system. They are the little fences you put up to help your life feel the way you want it to feel. And to help you live your life and show up the way you want to show up within it.

Once, I was working as a personal trainer and managing a lot of areas. I always found more work to do, if you have your own business, or if you love your job, because you constantly keep finding work to do, right? I found I was starting work at 4 am and I would easily not be finished until 6 or 7 pm. Easily, I just kept working. But then I started to find I couldn't sleep because my brain would just keep going. My anxiety started to peak, and my life began to suffer so I paid attention to the feelings about what wasn't working for me. And that was I was working way too bigger days, and far too late into the night for my melon. So, I created a boundary for myself, for my working life and private life. The computer got shut at 4 pm. That's it. Like, done. No matter what was going on I created that boundary for myself.

You can create a boundary with anything in your life, anything at all. If ensuring your needs are being met whilst also honouring the needs of the people you love. Boundaries are essential.

If you're still not sure where you need one, it helps to examine what we tolerate for starters. If a situation keeps coming up for you and you're not feeling good about it—those feelings are your signal—that's something worth having a look at.

I know many new mums have several visitors. For instance, people might come in constantly, turning up and you may start feeling really encroached upon. Work out where a situation is not feeling aligned for you, then create a little rule for yourself that will support you in maintaining a feeling you *do* want that protects the way you feel. You protect your space, you protect your energy, and you know where to draw the line. And you know you can then communicate these loving boundaries with those you love and care about. That's actually the point. If you have lots of people constantly dropping in at the house, and that's not making you feel very good, then you can communicate effectively, calmly and concisely that. 'Hey, Janet, can you text me before you come around to see the baby?' 'We'd love to see you, but please text first.' If they text, then you get to decide if it's a good time or not. Once you work out where a boundary needs to go, you need to acknowledge it and action it. That will firstly mean getting clear on what it is and lovingly outline it when the situation arises.

A question I see come about for people in changing the way they do things is the fear of how others will perceive them and their new line in the sand.

'But, what if they get mad or they don't understand?'

Again, another epic question. You will love this one I just know it. We need to put our big girl panties on and we need to look at our *why*. Why are we creating these boundaries or these little life guides in the first place? Your *why* is the reason you created this loving little life fence in the first place, right? Right.

I will continue with the new baby at home for a second because we're on a roll. If you've got a new baby at home, you want to bond with your baby. You want to allow your baby to sleep; you want to know who is coming into your home, so you can decide how you feel about it. If that will suit you guys. And you want to decide whether a visitor will interrupt your routine or whatever it is you have with your baby. Your boundary is people have to let you know if they plan to come over first. Your *why* is all the reasons just listed. Whenever it comes to gently or assertively enforcing your boundary, you know in the back of your mind *that* is your why and if you're strong enough in your why, you can execute any *how*.

In your relationships, perhaps, the relationship with your romantic partner for instance. If there's an instance or circumstance that keeps coming up for you and you're feeling less than or simply don't like the way you're feeling, pinpoint it. Work out where it's coming from and what you can do to better handle yourself and your vibes within that.

Work out where the issue is coming from, acknowledge it.

Then work out what you want to do and create the rule and the guideline for how you want to live your life.

Then lovingly ensure that it's met.

> *"My boundaries weren't created to offend you,*
> *they were created to honour me."*
> **Unknown**

Let's look at another example of a boundary. You have dedicated a day entirely to you and taking care of all your needs. Self-care Sunday, and you're pumped about it. This Sunday will be your day. And then Susan from Accounting asked you to organise a company barbecue and your mother-in-law wants you to bring over your specialty dish for some weird cousin or whatever it is. You get the call. Check in with yourself, you'll know whether that's encroaching on your boundary. You'll know whether that will serve you and whether that will lift you up or pull you down and then you have the choice.

What's your why?

Your why is, I am needing this Sunday for myself, so I can then show up on Monday refreshed, with a full self-care cup and give to my family and loved ones from that overflow. So, you might lovingly have to say, 'Really sorry, I can't. Thank you anyway, but no not this weekend.'

That's it.

But then the hamster wheel of guilt and negative thoughts start. *I have to do this because if I don't they will be mad.* Fear arrives.

What's the fear making you say yes? What's the fear, the underlying belief: If I don't do this, they won't love me. *If I don't do this, they won't like me. If I don't do it their way, then I'm not going to be seen as valuable and they will get mad.*

Is a relationship based on fear, guilt, and obligation one you want to be in? If they aren't willing to accept your 'no' and they judge you for it, or if they will hate you for it, if they think all these things . . . Then let them think that and let that be a sign for you that they're not your people.

We do not create a boundary to offend someone else; it's created to honour you.

We do not create a boundary to piss someone else off; it's created to honour your needs.

We do not create a boundary to be a wall to block everyone out.

We create a boundary to protect and keep sacred all that you hold dear, and that is a beautiful loving boundary.

Boundaries, they're not put in place to shut us off or to make it unreasonable. We implement them and we decide on them because they will make our life better.

What do we do if someone is not respecting our boundaries and keep encroaching on our boundaries? Well, again, we have to put our big girl panties on and work out why this is happening, why we are allowing it to happen. And we need to examine what we tolerate. We need to take ownership of what we are allowing in our lives. We need to take ownership of the patterns we are part of. We need to take ownership of our ability to change and pivot, and of course, correct a bazillion times throughout our life and own it. It's not, 'Oh, but they just keep coming over.'

Yeah, I'm not buying what you're selling.

The most important promises you will ever keep, all the ones you make to yourself, that's your foundation. The promises we make to ourselves are our foundation for everything. If we crap out on our goals to ourselves, our desires to ourselves, our promises to ourselves, what pattern does that set up for the rest of our lives?

If we say we're going to no longer work after 5 pm, but we don't leave the office at 5 pm, we leave at 7 pm, we leave at 8 pm and then we are feeling miserable. that's on us.

That's on us.

If we say from now on if you have something planned and you've written it in your diary for yourself, you will put yourself first, right? Do this if you have your self-care Sunday or self-care Saturday, or you have a massage booked or whatever, and someone's going to ask you to do something in that time. If you get the call from them and you say, 'Oh, yes, okay, I will,' then you resent them for it. We need to take ownership of our place in our story. We need to take ownership of why we're blurring the lines and why we feel it's acceptable to say, no to our soul, and yes to someone else. How do you think that will make your soul feel? Shit house, it will make you feel shit house! That's just a given.

It's not your mother's-in-law or your mother's fault for asking you to do it. It's your fault for saying yes when you really wanted to say no.

Who has just got mad at me a little then? I even got a little mad at me then because it's true and sometimes the truth can be triggering. We need to own our own place in our story. And the only way we will move forward, more often than not, is when we get sick and tired of our own BS stories we're telling ourselves.

How do you keep your boundaries? You honour them.

You honour them.

How do you communicate effectively that these boundaries are in place?

You know your why.

You get crystal freaking clear, on your why and you own that.

No is a complete sentence.

You don't owe anyone an explanation. Try this on for size. I will give you five ways to say no without sounding like a biatch.

'No, thank you. I can't this weekend.'

'No, but thanks anyway.'

'Sorry, I can't, but have a great time.'

'I'll pass this time, but thanks for asking.'

'That sounds great, but it's really not my thing.'

Then when you get a little more confident.

'Yeah, nah. Not keen.'

'Not for me thanks, but good luck with that.'

'I'd rather put a fork in my eye, but you enjoy yourself.'

'I wish I could, but I don't really want to.'

'Sharon, that sounds like a nightmare. No, thanks.'

It's simple. If they ask again and push the fact, keep your response short and sweet. Whatever it is, own it, own it, own it. And you know what? No, might piss them off. But it will most definitely set you free. If someone keeps encroaching on your boundaries, you are the one who has the choice. Stay stuck or take a solid look and examine what you tolerate. Crystal freaking clear communication is the key to maintaining loving boundaries and you are so capable of making some.

The only reason someone will have
a problem with

your boundary

is if they try to cross them.

42.

INTROVERTED EXTROVERT

What *is* an introvert? I used to think it was someone who was shy, reserved or even a bit of a recluse. That was until I became a student of my emotions and realised something profound. I am one.

> According to Introvert, Dear, the definition of an introvert goes something like this;
>
> **'Introvert Definition:**
>
> *The definition of an introvert is someone who prefers calm, minimally stimulating environments. Introverts tend to feel drained after socializing and regain their energy by spending time alone. This is largely because introverts' brains respond to dopamine differently than extroverts' brains. In other words, if you're an introvert, you were likely born that way.*

Hot dang. There's a name for it and it explains why after every big event, launch, speaking commitment or even some meetings, I crash and need alone time before I *people* again. I had always thought that because I love connecting with people and I do what I do, that would make me an extrovert. Buzzer sounds . . . errrrrrrrrr, wrong.

I am more of an introvert and it explains so flipping much to me. Curious to learn more? I thought I would bring in an amazing woman who knows more about introverts than anyone I know and celebrates the fact we do life a little differently.

Katherine Mackenzie Smith runs an amazing podcast called The League of Extraordinary Introverts, so I knew she would definitely have some great words to share on this topic. I asked Katherine if there was an exact moment she realised she was an introvert and how it showed up for her.

> "It's so funny because I have no recollection of when or how I knew, it's just something I always knew. When I first started working for myself, I was talking with my coach about my business and the subject of being an introvert came up, probably as an excuse to not do something she was suggesting!"

Turns out, it's just something Katherine's always known.

> "I started my career working in the bustling television industry where my introversion became very apparent. Not only was I exhausted by the end of a shoot, I just never really fit in with the super outgoing personalities. When I started working for myself it was like something just clicked into place. I get to

dictate my schedule, how many people I need to talk to, and what I need to thrive in my own business."

In her personal life, because of the super successful work Katherine does, her nearest and dearest understands what she needs. It lets her off the hook a lot in terms of which events she attends and how she spends her day. Don't you just love that? Unapologetically caring for your own energy!

> "By far the biggest misconception is that introverts don't like people. The reality is most introverts are just mindful of quality over quantity and are looking for deep and meaningful connection. You're most likely going to find a couple of introverts sitting having a deep conversation in a quiet cafe than out at a party with hundreds of people.
>
> Having said that, I think we all have a switch that flicks at some point when interaction becomes too much. And the point determines where you are on the spectrum between introvert and extrovert. A highly introverted person might be able to manage 10 minutes in a large group. And a highly extroverted person might last 10 hours, but at some point, everyone needs to get away for some alone time."

Preeeeeach! 'We are all so, so different.' What one person would find invigorating, another may find draining. The key is knowing what personally floats your boat and recharges your batteries then ensuring you honour that. Curious, as always, I asked Katherine how she honours what she needs and to continually show up as her best self and I've got to tell you, I want what she's having.

> "Quality sleep, quiet mornings, and managing my energy are my non-negotiables. Luckily, I get the first two because I work from home and live with someone who is out of the house most mornings at 4 am."
>
> I've invested a lot of time this year learning more about my energy and nervous system to be able to have the emotional and energetic bandwidth to deal with stress better, have better boundaries, and feel less overwhelmed around lots of people—all things that I highly recommend!"

There's one of my absolute fav words and tools right there: boundaries. Woot-woo! I also know Katherine has a great energy gathering exercise for anyone who feels they could use some extra support, so check her out at katherinemackenziesmith.com/energy

Here's the thing I was super curious about too. Introverted extroverts. Like, I love being around people and connecting with everyone on stage, but then I need to retreat and recharge. I asked her is there such thing as an introverted extrovert?

> "Another huge misconception about introverts and extroverts is that you're either one or the other. The reality is that we all sit on a spectrum, originally identified by Carl Jung. Most tests gauge it on a scale of extroversion, so we are all a percentage of that (from memory, I'm about 13% extrovert.) To be honest, this can change depending on the circumstances, people around me, my mood, and even the time of month or year).
>
> Most people will identify as more introverted or more extroverted, simply meaning we gain more energy from time spent alone, or time spent with others. And then there is the sweet spot in the middle, often referred to as 'ambiverts'.

Technically, an introverted extrovert is a made-up term for someone who identifies closer to the middle of the scale, but more on the extrovert side. And I guess, an extroverted introvert would fall just on the introvert side."

Well, there you have it! We can be both, we already are and working out what fuels you might just be your golden ticket to a whole new way of doing things.

What's not to love about that!

It's okay to piss them off
if you're honouring what you need.

43.

SAY 'YES' TO THE DRESS

My goodness society puts a lot of pressure on marriage and the importance of all the trimmings that come along with it. For anyone who's getting married, has been married, or is hoping to get married one day, we all know we think about the dress. We all think about the dress and what it will look like. We think about how we'll walk down the aisle, and what he will think when he sees us. We wonder how it will photograph and the shoes and the flowers; we think about everything obviously, but the dress is usually the hero.

> **Can you think about a moment in your life where you put so much focus on a material thing?**
>
> **Was it a picture, perhaps? Rug? Handbag?**
> **Or even some jewellery?**

My wedding dress was beautiful. I just put my wedding dress in a plastic bag. Seriously, a plastic bag. A dress that hung like a trophy the day of my wedding up on the curtain railing with the light behind it was just put in a plastic bag. I folded it, this beautiful dress, this expensive beautiful dress just folded, rolled, and put in a plastic bag with the air pressed out of it just like the organisation requested, and posted it away.

    Just like that. Gone.

My wedding dress went to a beautiful organisation called Angel Gowns Australia. Angel Gowns turn wedding dresses into gowns for babies born way, way, way too soon who we lose, for stillborn babies, and babies who were just too wonderful for this Earth. When a family lose a baby and they need a gown for it to be buried in, or however that family chooses for their baby to pass over, they call Angel Gowns and Angel Gowns send one to them, so they don't have to think about that on top of everything else. I wondered what to do with my wedding dress for a while. I've been divorced almost two years and on the first anniversary of that I was all, *I need to think of something to do with this dress*. A dress that at one point meant so much to me. It didn't feel right to sell it. It didn't feel right to give it to someone to 'trash the dress' for a photoshoot or anything, but I knew as soon as I came across Angel Gowns, it was the most beautiful thing I could possibly hope for that dress. Even though the marriage didn't end the way I expected, the dress can go on to take a little burden off some families who are just going through too much. Too much to even comprehend.

The whole process really forced me to get honest.

Obviously, there's the whole element of how I can't imagine what those families are going through. That breaks my heart and I am so grateful for my healthy cubs.

The thing that shocked me like a finger in an electrical socket was just how much emphasis I had placed, and *we* place on the material being like the dress. Something that held so much of my interest and so much pressure around to end up in a plastic bag and posted away. This symbol of whatever I created for it to be was virtually rolled into a ball and sent away. The tissue paper from the box I had it carefully placed in was flying everywhere. I had treated this dress and was saving it as a symbol. When really all it was, was a dress. A dress I'd placed meaning, expectations and a story upon. This blew my mind. The importance we place on material things more often than not is fucked. This was my freaken wedding dress and look where it ended up. It was time for me to let it go and in doing so let a question mark for me become a full stop for someone else.

The lesson for me came in the invitation to look at the story and the emphasis and importance we're putting on different elements of our life. We need to make sure it matches up. We need to make sure that shit we are deeming to be so flipping important is actually what's important after all. It just goes to show things can come and go. They come into our lives, we let them go from our lives, but the important thing is the effect we have on those we love, the effect in the memories we make. For me, knowing I left more moments changed for the better than ones I wished I could change.

I still loved the dress, you know. I still absolutely loved the dress, but it didn't mean what it once did to me, but it definitely meant something letting it go.

Every relationship will change you. My marriage, or lack of one now, has highlighted the things that are important, and what things will symbolize for me in the future. Like a marriage certificate, for someone who's divorced now and everything that went on there, a marriage certificate won't have the same meaning as what it used to. Being in a relationship where we choose each other day in and day out, regardless of piece of paper, that's the magic that's important to me now.

That's the real deal.

That, I want.

That act of choosing each other means more to me than a marriage certificate. But I wouldn't have had that realisation if I hadn't walked the path I did and that's not to say I don't believe in marriage. I believe everyone has the right to have an amazing relationship, however that looks and feels for them. This is not so much about my wedding dress but more about the attachment and the importance we are so often unaware we place on material items, or items that can be taken away far too easily.

The order of importance of the things we give within our life. I know for sure we talked a lot about the decorations, the venue, the guest list and I know there was a lot of deliberation over the wine list. But I don't remember talking about our hopes and dreams for our relationship.

It's okay to want all the beautiful things in life, but I would hate to see them come at the expense of the quality things on your list.

Look at where you've prioritised and listed everything.

Does it match up on paper the way you'd like it to in your heart?

Are you giving airtime to the things that are really important in your life?

That list of yours, it's never too late to edit it.

Edit your life frequently and ruthlessly, and I hope you make some cool choices. I felt good about my choice for the new path of my dress.

Crazy, how things change.

Let it

change.

44.

DO YOU LIKE WHAT YOU SEE?

One of the biggest epidemics that effect our human condition is the way we view ourselves in this world.

    For real.

I bet if you asked most women, or others, if they love what they see in the mirror you'd get an overwhelming response of no's. This makes me sad.

How do you feel when you look in the mirror at your reflection?

Are you building yourself up or pulling yourself to pieces?

Imagine if you accepted and embraced what you see?

Until the trip to Byron Bay, I thought I had an okay body image with a few hiccups here and there, obvs. But the truth is I can spot a flaw on my body a mile away. At home, I don't have a mirror that allows me to see past shoulder height. Up here there's a mirror in the bathroom that gets a tonne of natural light, so nothing is sacred—read: avoided. I get full view of my caesarean scar. I get the full monty experience and see angles I'd rather not and some outfits I felt rather good about myself in had me questioning what I was putting in my coffee. Oh, yeah, I'm back having a cup a day and I love it.

I am a smallish person, just under 5'7" tall and I'm not drastically overweight but I know when I feel comfortable in my clothes and when I've been moving my body and eating well, that's generally the case but it's a fine line for sure. For this trip I dusted off the 'kinis to venture out amongst the young and tanned tourists of the world. And I became increasingly aware of my so-called *flaws*. All of a sudden, my hernia started to bug me, the cellulite I have bought up feelings of undesirability. And the knowledge I would always fall back on was the fact I had okay boobs, and they would make up for all the other less appealing features. Oh, shit, that's right, they are about to be on the floor of an operating theatre very soon.

    Ai, Ai, Ai.

I had to sort my shit out and start placing my worth and my emphasis on what really matters pretty effing quick. Because when they go, my ability to back myself according to this conversation I was having becomes pretty shady.

    The fork in the road was clear, and I had to choose.

    I had to choose what I would value about myself.

    I had to choose what I would prioritise about being on the beach.

I had to choose what my changed appearance would mean for me in that very moment, on the sand, and for every moment thereafter.

Feeling *worthy* is a choice.

Feeling *beautiful* is a choice.

Feeling *comfortable* in your own skin is a choice.

Deciding to be *enough* is a choice.

Choosing what to focus on is a choice.

Have you ever wondered how some people can just do things so much easier? You know the people who just walk down to the beach without a sarong, stand up in front on hundreds of people without a second thought? Or how some people can walk into a room and start a conversation with anybody?

They choose it.

They choose to believe in themselves and they choose to believe they are worth it.

Yes, I, 100% acknowledge some people will be reading this and saying things are harder for them because they weigh *this* much or look *this* way, but the choice is still there.

It is always a choice and let's not for a second pretend it's not. If you have ever lost a bunch of weight thinking it would make you happy, got to the goal and realised you're still forking miserable then you know this is true. You will be happy enough within yourself when you choose to be content within yourself. Someone should put that on a bumper sticker!

We are so much more than our body's and the way our skin looks.

We are the way we light up when we talk about the things we love.

We are the kindness we offer to others.

We are the laughter we create in a room.

We are the warm hugs, the shoulder to lean on and the reason today was so great for someone.

We are the mischief makers, that friend of someone's and the ones who make inappropriate jokes.

We are the life givers, the life shapers and the magic makers.

We are the ones who rescue snails on the path.

We are the ones who marvel at the stars and the one who can always be trusted.

If we spend our time focussing on superficial shit upon our surface, we will never know the beauty of our depths.

It's a choice.

It's a choice.

It's a choice.

How do you move through it and change the way you view things? Sweetheart, you change the things you look for.

You get to

choose.

45.

I WILL WHEN I HAVE

Oh, if you could see me, you would see a major eye roll here. This one is a biggy. I know so many amazing women who put off their dreams because they believe life needs to look a certain way before they can go ahead and do the *thing*. They believe we need to be a certain person before we can live a certain path. We convince ourselves we need to be a certain type of person on our path before we are able to take the next step. So many amazing women have a goal to write a book, yet almost every single person who desires to do so doesn't believe they have the potential to actually do it or they aren't the person they need to be in order to get it done.

Not true.

I have never done a writing course, taken a class or anything even remotely close to that which would signify I had been given permission to go forward to write a book. I just sat down in the chair and wrote it. It can be that simple when we stop waiting for permission to do something.

> **Is there an area of your life that you believe holds the key to your happiness?**
>
> **Are you allowing yourself to be happy and content before that or are you hanging all your joy on future plans?**

I'm friends with a couple who desperately wanted children, but he wouldn't move forward until they had $100,000 of savings in their account. Can you imagine how long that was going to take for them to accumulate that? That was the story he was telling himself however about what it was going to take to be able to provide for his family. Now, I'm not saying it was wrong, but it was certainly not essential to create a loving family. It's all about the story we hold around the thing and the belief system we carry with us about it.

When I first started coaching and became qualified, I still didn't feel like I had enough certifications to be of value to someone. This had nothing to do with my ability to be of value but more so my lack of belief in myself. I was scared I wasn't enough. I even looked at doing an incredibly expensive additional course in the hopes it would give me the emotional green light and certification to be able to go out there and encourage and coach people confidently.

Wrong answer.

The truth is, and this was told to me by my beautiful coach and mentor, Lauren Aletta, I didn't need another piece of paper to tell me I'm good enough. That worthiness needs to come from within. Plus, she also had a great point that just because something has amazing marketing attached to it doesn't mean I need it. It just means they have great marketing.

BOOM!

Sometimes we need someone to tell us how it is because our beautiful minds don't necessarily see things as they are. You don't need to be everything you think you need to be in order to do the things you want to do. You just need to decide that you want and do them.

That's it.

That's all it is.

And that, my friends, *is* enough.

We often think we need to become something else before we can begin, but it's in the beginning that helps us to become everything.

I discover my peace and solutions through writing about them. I rarely have an answer to a question before I begin. If you wish to become a world traveller, you can only do that by leaving the comfort of your couch. If you wish to have your own business, you are only going to fulfil that dream by creating and living life alongside your vision and your goals for that exact business. You will never become confident in heels by continuing to walk in flats. If you want to learn to ride a horse, you have to actually get your butt in the saddle. And if you want to be the one who achieves your dream then the first thing you have to believe is that you're ready and you are deserving.

Take a look at who you think you need to be in order to take the next step towards your dreams.

Now go stand in front of the mirror.

The person you see is the exact person you need to be in order to do *the* thing.

True story.

I already am.

46.

LAUGH IT OFF

I haven't laughed much in the last two years. Like really, laugh-so-hard-your-belly-aches kind of laugh. It's been survival mode here and I've had to run a tight ship to get us through the day. The kids had endless back-to-back sick times through winter. Frankly, I've had to compartmentalise my life for the fear looking at it too closely would bring me to my knees at times. We do what we have to do to get through what we have to get through and I'm proud of us for that. Yay. Go team.

While I am grateful for my life and I love the people in it, it can still get eerily dark here. Like scary dark. That little messenger is one I can't ignore. Constantly being the decision maker and responsible one can make you forget who you are and rob you of your JOY. I feel the weight of my life and the monotony of it often. It's easy for me to want to numb out from my feelings on Instagram at the end of another long day. That doesn't mean I didn't have beautiful moments within my day because I usually do. But in this chapter of my life I feel I'm having to work really, really hard to keep it altogether.

Am I happy?

Yes.

Am I tired?

Also, yes.

Do I feel overwhelmed?

Yes.

Would I change anything?

No.

I wouldn't even know what to change.

> **Do you ever have dark days in times of struggle?**
>
> **Are there times in your life when it feels like you're scooping poo out of a pond with a teaspoon?**
>
> **Do you stay in that space or search for a way out?**
>
> **When was the last time you put yourself in the path of your joy?**

I don't always get the balance right, and I hate having to ask my kids to be patient while Mummy sends an email for work or writes a post or takes a call. They don't understand it, but if Mummy doesn't run her business, then Mummy can't pay the bills. While I try to do it around their sleep schedules and daycare, sometimes it unavoidable and there's conflict.

We all have stuff. We're all fighting a battle in secret and what I know for sure is no one really has their shit together. Like, ever. There will be pockets of time where life flows beautifully but there will also be pockets of life where the laughter doesn't fill the walls like we wished it would.

That's life though.

Some chapters evoke laughter.

Some make us work for it.

Some rob us of it.

I so desperately want to be one of the mums at a BBQ having a cocktail, singing out loud with their kids running around their feet. I want to be that carefree woman but the weight of the responsibility of it *all* usually takes the fun out of it for me. I don't know what the answer is, but I'm fairly sure allowing space for play and joy is part of the answer. I don't know how many times I have wanted to say yes to something, but the amount of 'hard' it would bring up for me in my world had me running the other way. Being the solo Mumma of two beautiful little wildlings is always my number one priority so if something impedes me from doing the best I can, I struggle to find the yes. Or, I do manage to say yes, and the boys become unwell. Or, work pops up. Or, someone else changes the schedule and a life of possibility feels even more out of reach than ever. We can't stop here. We can't stay parked here on the corner of lost and confused. We need to stay open. We need to be willing and we need to toss the what-ifs out the window sometimes and just see what happens.

I know it's a constant mathematics equation when you're a parent. Every choice we make has two aspects and we have to weigh it up. How much fun will this be for me vs how difficult will it be to have the kids looked after + (plus) the guilt I will feel for not being with my kids = (equals) the perception in my mind about what this will say about me as a mother.

The math is real.

I'm not sure men have this same tortured relationship with allowing room for joy within their lives. I don't think they think about it as hard. As women we love a backstory. We can't just go out for dinner; we have to do the maths. Men seem to walk out the door and enjoy their meal. Now, I'm not a man so I guess I'm generalising here, but I still think I'm bang on. Women plan, think and then carry that weight with them for some time, and I've got to tell you, I think we just need to get out of our own forking way.

Let's give ourselves permission to let it be easy. This weight we place on our backs isn't always ours to carry. I know we think by worrying about it and stressing over it we feel like we are doing something proactive towards making things easier but all it is doing is making things harder. All the worry is doing is robbing you of a chance at some feel good vibes. So, next time someone asks you to go somewhere or do something, before you talk yourself out of it, say *yes*.

Put yourself in the path of fun.

Let yourself be a little random.

Say yes to friends and spontaneous adventures because chances are they will remind you who you are, and who you are is worth remembering.

This I know, for sure.

Who

you are

is

worth remembering.

47.

I AM WILLING

Life is truly a mixed bag. Alongside the wonderful parts, the joy, the magic, and the gifts, we will each face hurdles, challenges, grief, loss. The confusion as to how we will navigate them can be immense. Our ability to face whatever life throws at us depends on one thing, whether we are willing to carry on.

We have to be willing to carry on.

All we ever have to do to navigate life's hurdles and the sticky situations, is to evoke the right mindset with these three little words: I am willing.

> **Can you imagine how different it would feel if you didn't believe some feelings were wrong or unwelcome?**
>
> **How would it feel to welcome all feelings instead of just the warmer ones?**

It doesn't even have to be the huge life altering situations that bring you down either. I'm going to throw this right out there now for y'all and bring some period talk up in these pages.

If you haven't started charting your cycle and paying attention to the way your energy, mood and overall feelings will shift throughout your days, you'll be forking mind blown. I only ever charted my cycle to see when I was ovulating to fall pregnant. But I was missing out on some of the most useful information about my life and what is possible and best to schedule. At the time of writing this I have been charting my energy levels and emotions for around three months and it astounds me that I am that predictable. That I didn't know about this before. That I have that many days where I'm predisposed to feeling a little low vibe. Honestly, I take a good six days (day one is the start of your period) so days one to six of my cycle, I'm like, not great. Energy-wise I feel really low and my vibes are all *meh* and that's totally normal for your cycle because I'm in my winter phase. Today, I'm on day seven or eight, which is my spring phase, because we're all sharing here. The inspiration's coming back, the focus is returning, and I am feeling all sorts of these rad new vibes.

I couldn't get to this delicious part of my new everything if I wasn't willing to allow myself to feel a little rotten for a few days. You're probably thinking, *Dang, girl, you don't really have a choice with your moons; they are coming whether you like it or not.* True. This would be true, but I totally have a choice in the way I'll allow myself to experience them.

    That, my friend, is the ticket.

    I am willing.

Next time you catch yourself feeling all the feels, struggling with the big struggles and you first noticed it all, that is your invitation to a choice of how you wish to proceed.

Acknowledgement of how you're feeling gives you the opportunity to acknowledge what you're going through and how to figure it out. Question why are you feeling this way? Then come to a realisation. From there, you've got options. You can fight it, you can avoid it, you can sit there stuck in it and hating it or you can be willing to let it do its job.

I am willing, is your mantra to meet that hurdle.

I am willing to feel this pain.

I am willing to embrace this, tune in and give myself what it needs.

I am willing to keep showing up for myself.

I am willing to experience this part of my life with my eyes open.

I am willing to have this pain as a receipt of the fact that I loved so deeply.

I am willing.

As long as you have the *will*, as long as you are willing to keep keeping on and experiencing these feelings then, honey, you will be just fine because you have the *will* to do so. There are things that will go wrong, there's people who will let us down but how we choose to respond to that is everything. If we fight that and we get pissed at that for too long—obviously, we're human and we will react and respond to different things because sometimes people are just so people-y—we will prolong the process. Our option is instead, we give ourselves permission to carry on regardless, to carry on despite this and be willing to live our life with eyes open. The world will most likely make more sense and you become a willing participant rather than a hostage.

Doesn't it just feel better, that perspective, and that willingness is a choice.

Because we *always* have a choice.

I am

willing.

48.
IT'S NOT YOUR JOB TO BE EASY

I was making tea and listening to a movie playing in the background. A woman was worrying she will never find love because she's 'not easy to be with'. This made the hairs on the back of my neck stand up. Has someone ever told you that you are hard work, not easy to be with? We weren't put on this earth to make life easy for someone. There's no way how that could possibly be true.

I know many of us were raised with the conveyor belt dream of finish studying; find a man; settle down; get married; keep him happy; have the kids and you've reached a state or life of nirvana.

Yeah. Nah.

I do believe this timeline worked incredibly well for some people and if that's your goal now, power to you. The part that really got my goat is the 50s mentality of our purpose is to be likeable, not make waves and please others at all costs.

Fork that.

Fork that big time.

We have feelings, and it's okay for us to express them.

We have ideas and it's okay for us to share them.

We get hurt, and it's okay for us to cry.

We have dreams and it's okay for us to chase them.

We get tired and it's okay for us to rest.

We have a uterus and it's okay for us not to want to have children.

We have standards and it's okay for us to uphold them.

We are sensitive and it's okay for us to share that.

We might love you and it's okay for us to want to spend time with you.

We are mothers and it's okay for us to struggle with that sometimes.

We get mad, and if you don't know why we're mad then you don't know us at all—ha-ha—just kidding on that last one.

It's not our job to dim our light because it's shining in someone's eyes. The sun gives zero shits if it blinds you. We were not put on this earth to make things easy, but it will definitely going to help our case if we don't get about like a raging lunatic on the reg. Unless it's the first 5-6 days of your cycle, or maybe even days like 24-28. They are super dicey for me too. Okay, so there's a fair chunk of time where we may not be the easiest of people to be around, but I'm just going to quote Bob Marley here for you:

"If she's amazing, she won't be easy. If she's easy, she won't be amazing. If she's worth it, you won't give up. If you give up, you're not worthy. Truth is, everybody is going to hurt you; you just gotta find the ones worth suffering for."

Oh, Bob. I'm feeling you.

Our happiness on this earth is our own responsibility. No one can gift that to us. That's entirely on us. It's easy to want to expect our partners, family, or friends to make us happy but that's not how it works. Nagging also won't make you happy. Putting your expectations on to someone else won't make you happy—believe me. But being able to communicate your needs and doing what you can to make them a reality yourself is a move towards making you happy.

The same situation applies to others. We can't possibly wear the responsibility of making someone else happy. Let's retire from that. Flat out hang up our aprons to the role of attempting to make someone else happy. Done. Gone. Bye. We resign.

It's impossible.

Someone else's happiness has to come from them. I know, and trust me when I say, I *know* when you truly love someone; you want to do anything you can to please them.

Naaaaw, how sweet.

But turning yourself inside out to do so or betraying your own soul's needs in the process is a big old no deal. That is a recipe for burnout, resentment, and a lot of heartache. **We don't need to set ourselves on fire to keep others warm.** You can't live and love when you're ashes. It's not your job to be easy. It is your job to be you, and you, my friend, are more qualified AF— for that.

Stay away from those who make you feel like loving you is hard. They're *jerks.*

49.

JUST BECAUSE THEY BELIEVE IT, DOESN'T MAKE IT TRUE

Shut. The. Front. Door.

I came across this little quote on Pinterest today and I got all *Mmm hmm* . . . snaps fingers about it. Everyone will experience life in a different way. Everyone will have a different take on a set of events, and everyone will also have a different opinion of you.

That's okay.

I bet for some people that just made your chest a little tight. I get that.

> **Who or what comes to mind here?**
>
> **Have you at some point let someone else's opinion of you rank higher than your own?**

The fear of what people may think has kept me stuck in more situations than I care to admit. It's a really fearful place to be filled with low self-worth and it goes hand-in-hand with having your sense of self rest firmly in the opinions of others. Boooo to that. Yuck. Once I got to a place of giving way less shits about other people's perceptions of me, my confidence grew exponentially. Let's take a broken relationship. It's natural in any break up to worry about how everyone will perceive your place in it. *I wonder what they're saying to everyone? What if they think this was my fault? What if they are telling everyone lies?* Well, sweets, the bad news is hurt people, hurt people so if your ex is hurting and wants to save face then there's a really high chance he will throw you under the bus. A completely embellished bus.

    Again, this is okay.

Let people talk. Just as this title says, *just because they believe it, doesn't make it true!* Just because some people have a snapshot of you, doesn't mean they are privy to the entire picture. Just because someone runs their mouth, doesn't mean you need to run to defend yourself. When it comes down to it, people will believe whatever they want. Spending your precious life worrying about what *they* may or may not think of you is a super damaging way to spend your time.

    When you know the truth, what *they* think doesn't matter.

    When you know your why, what *they* think is irrelevant.

    When you back yourself, you don't owe anyone an explanation for anything.

    Zilch. Zip. Nada.

I know I had moments where I would hear things were being said, or I would worry about what people would think, but thankfully that passed real quick. Sure, I would acknowledge that's where my mind was going before course correcting. And I'd replace it with the knowledge my sense of self wasn't dependent on anyone else's perception of me and my choices.

Thank fork for that.

Look at where you're giving your power away right now. Whose opinion are you holding higher than your own? How's that working out for you? Now you know, you can set yourself free.

You're welcome!

Back
yourself.

50.

GETTING BIKINI BODY READY

Insert massive eye roll here. I will put my hand up to say as a personal trainer I know I used this slogan a lot, and the old 'summer bodies are made in winter' jam. I, we, did so because we knew it was a situation we could all relate to and I still acknowledge that within myself. These days I like to call it eating seasonally and intuitively. There's so much forking guilt placed on women around what we eat and how we're meant to look. I'm not sure when it changes but I know as we grow wiser and become a student of our emotions and actions, we realise there's a shitload more to life than the way we look.

Healthy looks different for every *body*.

This summer I feel more confident in a bikini than I ever have before, even though it doesn't fit the ideal society pushes on us.

> **How do you feel in a swimsuit?**
>
> **Have you ever succumbed to pressure to get bikini body ready?**
>
> **How great would it be to understand your body and accept it? Regardless?**

I'm currently four weeks post-surgery and let's just say there's a lot going on to look at. Where I had my tummy surgery is doing something weird and still healing. Imagine a banana sitting under the skin above my belly button . . . you're getting close, plus, I have tape under each boob holding the incisions closed from the explant surgery. To give you an idea two giant strips of white masking tape under each bozzy. I know, I know, hot right?

I really and truly don't care though.

It doesn't matter. None of it. The lumps, bumps and soon to be scars don't matter. How we *feel* does, and I feel great!

> We are so much more than our birthday suits!
>
> We are hearts and twinkling eyes.
>
> We are friends and mothers and sisters.
>
> We are sensual and cheeky.
>
> We are laughter and sensitivity and strength.
>
> My body has endured and I'm guessing yours has to.

Sure, I have moments where insecurities creep in around being desirable or attractive, but people who mind don't matter, and people who matter don't mind. No number of hours in the gym, clean eating or hectic runs will give you what you can gift yourself right now. Permission to feel worthy, loveable and all sorts of spicy!

You have to be willing.

You have to decide.

You change the story.

Instead of standing in front of the mirror picking yourself to pieces, you choose not to. Get your clothes on and if you've got nothing nice to say, carry on. If you catch a thought like, *how am I ever going to meet someone looking like this?* Meet it with compassion and reframe it. Try, *the right person will embrace me for who I am as soon as I am willing to embrace me for who I am.* Stop apologising for being who you are. When you allow yourself to be in your body you'll stop worrying about the world accepting you because you will have already accepted yourself.

If you notice that you are shaming yourself around food with words like, *here you go again, eating all the food,* or, *you shouldn't eat that, you're already fat enough.*

First, ouch.

That's really mean.

Second, fork that.

Food is just food.

Quit giving it the power to mean something more. Reframe it to something like, *I choose balance and I do so without the guilt.* Choose the foods that make you feel great and if eating a wheelbarrow load of cream buns does that then, lady, fill your boots. If it doesn't and you're doing it anyway, then that is a sign you're avoiding something or numbing out. Again, that's not wrong, it's just another signal or message you get to interpret. Pretty cool.

This year will feel pretty rad if you ask me, because I've chosen to come home to my body. My body is my home. While I don't look at my cellulite and think, *wow girl, that's so beautiful* I just don't attach to it because it just doesn't matter. I don't look at my lop-sided boobs and think, *geeeez what a rack*. But, I am okay with them. They really don't deserve too much thought. They are my breasts. That's it. Our bodies don't need judgement or appraisal.

They don't need to fit or be a certain size. Healthy is always a preference. I'm choosing to love the skin I'm in and not let the fear of how it looks be the reason I miss an opportunity to get amongst it this summer.

If you have a body, it's already a beach ready body!

You don't need to do anything. You don't need to lose weight or gain a perky butt. You could probably still get amongst the wax for that bikini line but if you are all about a full bush then babe, you do you.

There's so much debate about body hair as well these days but frankly it's fully your call. Grow it out, wax it off, braid it or bedazzle it. Whatever you want to roll with, rock it and rock it proudly. Whatever you choose to do with your body hair do it because you want to. And not because you think it's what you should be doing, or that someone has shamed you into thinking it's bad. The way I see it, we wouldn't have it if we weren't meant to. But just for the record, I do my best to keep those sideburns on my inner thighs under wraps. Just in case you were wondering. This took a turn, didn't it?

Carry on.

Just *do you.*

51.
THE GOOD GIRL MUST DIE

Blaaaaaah. I remember when my coach said this to me years and years ago. I was sitting on the couch in her lounge room and pouring out my heart and soul over all the perceived *bad* things I'd done and the guilt I was harbouring for them. She just stared at me blankly before shaking her head and exclaiming, 'The Good Girl Must Die.'

This was such a relief to me and was honestly the first step in realising the path is always the path and the best way to be in alignment is to slip off it. All my hungover Sundays—there's also been some Mondays, and definitely a few Saturdays and possibly some Thursdays—and not so wise choices thanks to whatever I was drinking haunted me. I knew that's not who I was, but I didn't have enough understanding to look a little deeper at what I was trying to run from. And I was also punishing myself for what turns out is actually the process.

> **Are you judging yourself somewhere for being human?**
>
> **Are you holding yourself accountable to an unattainable yard stick?**
>
> **How does that feel for you?**

I wasn't a bad person. I just wasn't doing the right thing by me. I wasn't making great choices always, but I wasn't a bad person because of the choices I was making.

We are loveable throughout all of our phases.

We are loveable when we are figuring it out.

We are worthy whilst we are making our best mistakes.

The notion you have to be the good girl to be deemed worthy, valuable or accepted is utter horseshit. This notion stinks so much I can smell it from here. This notion we always needed to walk a straight line as a good girl can stop you from realising your greatness.

I went to Catholic schools my entire school career, and they drummed it into me that good girls get rewarded and there's certain things only bad girls do. Obvs, the words were a little different, but they tainted this crazy and unrealistic path to sovereignty with impossible standards. It was also missing a giant part about embracing our whole selves.

What I've learnt is that it's okay to be both.

We need to be both.

Both is what makes us whole.

Let's lose the labels.

We don't need them. Instead of trying to fit into a box and stressing out if we spill out over the edges, let's remain fluid in our approach to life and curious to what we are always.

Women are sensual and beautiful beings. We are sensitive, intuitive and capable of magic. We are unexplainable, undefinable and as one of my favourite quotes says, 'We are the granddaughters of the witches they couldn't burn.' Doesn't that conjure up all the amazing witchy powers within?

If you've read *Becoming Brave*, then you would have been introduced to Ofa Fitzgibbons. She is one of my greatest friends, a soul I sit with in a circle on the reg. She's also one of the most wonderful women's empowerment and sensuality coaches I have ever come across. Ofa has this way of making you lean in and I knew when it came to this topic I had a few questions for her because of the way she unequivocally embraces her sovereignty. Ofa speaks so reverently about the connection we have with our body. We've had a conversation or two about the fact if you're out of touch with your body, there's a huge chance you're out of touch with another area of your life.

> "Our bodies are magical and wonderful things. I believe they are the custodians of our soul and spirit—our true essence—and how we physically show up in the world. They're also capable of telling us so much about who we are." Ofa continues. "I believe our bodies hold so much wisdom and tell us so much about ourselves that we have been taught to gloss over and sometimes ignore. Think about how your body tells you that you're nervous or stressed or in love. Typically, you get clammy

or sweaty hands combined with a butterfly sensation in the stomach, right?

What if you were to take that a step further? If you think about a specific milestone memory—like a birthday, significant family event, graduating high school—you can typically recall how you felt in that moment. Not only the emotions you were feeling but also how you held yourself, what you were wearing and how you felt in your body.

Unpacking sensations like these in the body—or lack of sensations—are essential to understanding our emotions and all the parts of ourselves.

It's a pathway to living a full life.

I've lived a lot of my life all up in my head. But as soon as I started bringing awareness to what my body wanted; what my body desired, I started feeling not only connected but ALIVE. I started feeling like life was juicy and one epic ride of awesome. Living an embodied life means living a life connected to what is going on in my body, rather than ignoring it.

One of the many roles of our womanly bodies is for reproduction and to keep life alive. But they are also a source of great feminine wisdom and sensuality.

I used to feel so disconnected to my womanly body. I was angry with it for so long because it wasn't giving me the one thing I wanted in life, a baby. So, I was shut down and shut off from these parts of me that were meant to create life and instead, felt disconnected from life.

As soon as I started to connect with my womanly body, fully and on a daily basis—my womb and my breasts just to a name a couple—the pain, anger and frustration started to melt away. Once I moved through these emotions, I started feeling more feminine, more sensual and definitely more alive.

For me, the body/mind is an integrated concept. Not two separate ones, the body and the mind. As a colleague once explained to me, we hold issues in our tissues so it's important to listen to what our bodies are trying to tell us."

I asked Ofa why she thought many women find themselves disconnected from themselves, here's what she had to say.

"Unfortunately, I think there are many reasons. Fear from being seen. Traumatic life events. Running from pain. Running from who we truly are.

We live in a society that has discouraged women to fully embrace who we are and to connect to our whole selves. We are taught our sexual desires and expression are wrong. We can be labelled frigid or repressed if we don't feel safe to explore our sexuality; or a slut if we want to experience sexual freedom. We are surrounded by messages of how we should look, think and feel.

I think a lot of this disconnection isn't overt. I don't think we wake up one morning and think 'Hey, I'm gonna feel disconnected to my body today. YAY ME!' But I do think things like the way we are brought up, our family values and what we were taught at home, how our primary caretakers took care of us has a huge impact on how we connect with ourselves.

For example, I grew up in a Christian household to beautiful, loving parents. But we never talked about sex and sexuality. Throughout high school I learned from books, friends, some school classes and then through my own exploration. But for so long I held a lot of shame about sex. That sex was evil and bad, and I would die and go to hell. Reflecting on that time and into my early twenties, I believe shame manifested itself in a number of ways including some physical issues with my womb and acknowledging a repressed part of my identity that was too afraid to do anything. While this seem may seem heavy—and don't get me wrong, it certainly felt heavy at the time I was processing all of this—I share this because the integration of this all has been such a wonderful softening of my heart. I feel more open to receiving love more deeply and freely than ever before.

I think the silver lining to this grey cloud of disconnection is this, we live in a time where we are becoming more empowered to find out our true selves. There's a sexual revolution happening where there is a wealth of information about how we can live life in a more connected way.

For me, feeling disconnected to my body is often a result of an event that has stayed with me in a way that has limited my aliveness and the fullness of love I want to express in my heart.

True story. I have always been 'the good girl'. A bit nerdy at uni, always participating in cultural events, being a good minister's daughter. I have always wanted to ACHIEVE, to be great at my job, to be a great friend/sister/wife/lover, to have success because I felt that's what I 'should' be doing. This was really present for me in my twenties. Seemingly everyone around me was doing the same. Getting promotions, starting successful businesses, having kids with the white picket fenced house.

I was striving for all of this, but something just didn't feel right.

And this 'feeling' was making me feel so exhausted and stressed.

Did I feel alive at the time? Truthfully, NO. I had three career burnouts plus years of self-medicated partying to prove it.

Did I express the fullness of love in my heart? Again, when I really think about this, I don't think I did. I don't think I really knew what the fullness of love actually meant. I had to go all the way to Mexico to find out what this meant.

In the Australian winter of 2017, I headed off on a tantra and embodiment retreat in Mexico. I hadn't attended a tantra retreat or been to Mexico before, so I was a bit apprehensive about what to expect. But I went with an open mind and heart, willing to push myself—to find my edge, if I felt safe—and to learn a thing or two. What I learned about myself on the first day has been a huge gift and will stay with me forever. I felt the full expression of pure love all through me. I could literally *feel* how every cell of my being was made up of tiny molecules of love. Through the simple practice of meditation, focus and breathwork, I could sense an explosion of soft electricity out of my chest and around my body, fusing this electricity with universe. It was a pretty mind-blowing experience!

Hindsight really is a beautiful thing. I can look back at this time during my twenties now with a lot of fondness and mature eyes rather than sadness at how lost I seemed. If my twenties were all about FREEDOM, then my thirties have been all about FINDING ME."

I asked Ofa what some great ways are to reconnect and nurture the relationship we have with our bodies, here's what she had to say:

"There are a number of ways women can reconnect with themselves. In my personal practice, these are my go-to's:

1. Paying attention to body sensations (or the felt sense)

    I like to do this while meditating. Rather than just trying to focus on clearing my thoughts, I like to drop into my body and notice what sensations come up for me. Sometimes I say these out loud, sometimes I say them in my mind. Either way, it's a beautiful practice to help bring awareness to what's going on in my body.

2. Breathwork

    I absolutely LOVE breathwork. Connecting with the felt sense and breath really helps to soften into more body awareness and connection.

3. Dancing!

    I believe our bodies are meant to move to music. There's something special about putting on a song and really feeling the music and allowing it to move through your body.

4. Sexuality practices

    Sexuality practices are a beautiful way to connect with the body. Our heteronormative society still largely portrays women's bodies as being tools to pleasure men. We are not usually taught to seek out what pleasure means in our bodies as women. A regular self-pleasure practice including things like a yoni/jade-egg practice and breast massage are great ways to connect with your body."

Thank you, Ofa. I mean, wow! Could you be guided into fostering a more loving relationship with your vessel? I think not. Our bodies are so much more than the way we get around. They are capable, magnificent and wise beyond our comprehension. Shame and guilt can impede that and what a pity it would be to go through life holding on to something that was never yours to carry.

Your body is beautiful, it's okay to feel desired and be desirable and your sensuality is part of your spirit. It's our essence and part of who we are. There's absolutely nothing to be hidden about that.

End scene.

52.

A WOMAN'S WORTH

Is immeasurable.

Carry on.

There's no such thing as a woman's worth.

She just is.

53.

ALL EYES ARE ON YOU

Okay, so this is a pretty important piece of the puzzle and I have a question for you: What are you doing to make it happen? Seriously, though, we all have these huge dreams, these grandiose aspirations, these inspiration boards filled with pins but how many of us are doing something to get us there?

Here's another question: What have you stopped doing that you loved and made you feel like you? Same thing! I don't know why we do it, I just know that so often we want the outcome, but we unconsciously prioritise everything else above it and no longer do the work. Or we stop doing the things that light us up and then wonder why it's so dark out. It's our responsibility as the divine co-creator of this life to actively play a part in the way it will pan out. We can't control the outcome, but we can mother trucking collaborate with the universe and pull our weight!

Today, a writing contract of mine finished up, and there were moments of *uh-oh, now what am I going to do?* That was a large portion of my stable weekly income and I relied on that for you know, groceries and stuff. I procrastinated and hung sheets for curtains, vacuumed up sand from the floor, folded the washing, complained about some random things to my mum and stopped dead in my tracks. I'm writing a forking book, that's what I'm doing. I'm going to channel my efforts into that and make a little magic on my own terms.

It's up to me!

Just like it's up to *you*!

Here's what I have just figured out. I have to put my butt in the chair and articulate the lightning bolt of inspiration so it's not lost in the cosmos. I want to connect with amazing women and support them whilst they do all sorts of epic things whilst seeing the world differently. That means I have to do something that will help me do that. I want financial security, so I have to do the things that will help me gain financial security.

I trotted over to my laptop and opened it up. Actually, no, it wasn't that simple. I had to pry one of those child safety guards out of the socket with a knife which was as dangerous as it sounds. Untangle the extension cord, find the right bits and pieces in my bag, try to plug it into my computer, realise it's upside down and turn it over again. And then after all that's done, and I've got a little boob sweat happening, I could sit to write this chapter. Why? Because, important. If we want the outcome, we have to do the work. Consider this your loving kick in the butt to own your choices. If we want to be successful, we have to continually show up. There's no silver bullet to making your dreams come true except for consistently pulling your finger out and making a step or two towards your goal.

You. Are. Welcome!

This question, of course, is a pearler!

> **What have you stopped doing that you loved that helped you feel like you?**

I'm not sure why we do it but when the going gets tough, our go to is to usually toss off all the things that help us feel like sunshine. We're real sickos like that. The exercise stops because you're too busy. The meditation ceases because your mind is too noisy. You feel like shit because you eat shitty foods. Your relationships suffer because you're stressed out, feel like shit and haven't exercised in weeks. You see what's happening here? You stop doing the things; you stop feeling the things. These simple tools and tricks we have at our fingertips don't work their magic by accident. They work their magic on us because that's what our souls need.

Imagine for a second you kept up with your art classes or your long walks through a crazy stressful time.

Imagine ensuring you're eating well and prioritising sleep when you are working towards a deadline or your children all go through a phase for like, five years.

Imagine if you took the time to peace out or take a boxing class instead of using your partner as a verbal boxing bag. I'm guessing the outcome would be decidedly different or let's even say marginally better.

It's time to get really honest with yourself girlfriend.

What have you stopped doing that makes you feel the way you want to feel?

Are you doing the things that will give you the most bang for your buck in life and business? If you're not, could you? Do you know what they are? The relationship you have with time and the way you spend it is so flipping important. Have a think about that for me.

Perhaps it's so dark because you've stopped *doing the things that light you up?*

54.

HIGH HOPES

One thing I have learnt from this life is that hope is the key to so much.

Hope and a belief in something more than ourselves. It's a belief in our future, a belief and a wish for love and the faith that everything will turn out okay sets you up for things to, in fact, turn out okay.

What you tell yourself matters.

How you talk to yourself matters.

What you choose to believe in matters.

What you breathe in, share throughout the world—it matters!

Your belief about what you deserve, what is coming for you and what you can bring to the world really forking matters. There will be times where it hurts, or they leave, or you feel you have lost everything, and you will doubt it all. One day, the time will be right, and you'll come back to *hope* and see your grief as a receipt for having loved so big and so hard. In that moment you will be filled with light and with faith in life again.

When you realise you are the one who determines how you experience anything and everything in this world, you will see the difference. Keeping hope in your heart is the difference between a shitty day and a day that was challenging but part of something more.

When you have hope in your heart, you will embrace the days alone because you know that what's meant for you won't pass you by.

You will know that every day brings new possibilities.

You will smile for no reason.

You will see the bees on the flowers at the beach.

You will feel the breeze on your face.

You will enjoy every last bit of that burger.

You will sleep diagonally across the bed.

You will take more chances.

You will say yes to more adventures.

You will plan more picnics.

You won't focus on what you *don't* have, what you *do* have is already forking wonderful.

You will say yes to the extra vodka because you're having so much fun.

You will focus on what's great instead of what's not.

You will walk down the street and make eye contact with people.

You will be okay with no matter what comes your way because you have hope. And that, my friend, is a currency that can't be bought, but for those who have it they know it's going to be okay.

The last bit

Everything doesn't have to make sense for it to be wonderful. You're always the answer to the question. And I hope by now you realise you are a mother forking goddess capable of so much more than you realise. My wish, for you, is that you know that. That you know you are infinite possibilities wrapped in a human package. That you pivot, course correct, choose again and grab life by the ping pongs over and over again.

You are here because you matter.

You aren't stuck. You aren't lost.

You are ready, and I can't wait to hear about it.

Life doesn't have to make sense for it to be magical. The most magical parts make no sense at all. Life is one messy and simply complicated love storm and I am out here dancing with you in the rain.

Thank you, for allowing me into your heart and into your home, girlfriend. Until we meet again, may your days be filled with light breezes, rock star confidence and may the forks you give be for the things you love.

    Onwards.

About the author

KATIE DEAN a best selling author, motivational maven and the woman you want on your team.

Best selling author of *Becoming Brave,* Katie has guided thousands of women to debunk fear and shine a light in their lives on how to seek confidence, clarity and courage. She does all this whilst being a solo Mumma to two beautiful boys, the absolute loves of her life. With a refreshingly no BS approach, she uses an interactive speaking style, humour, her worldly insights and tools to take her audience on an epic path of bravery and self-discovery.

When you find yourself in the audience of one of Katie's events you know you are in for inspirationally filled with ah-ha moments that create real change.

Through her coaching, national speaking tours, live events and loved-up writing, she is hell bent on lighting people up, laughing loudly and has created a successful business to help women unearth their brave.

Resources

Thank you for doing this human-ing work and sharing these pages with me. It would be my honour for us to continue the shizzle and work together. There is magic in this messy life gig.

Brave Makers: Join the community for women creating their brave.

There is power in connection, you don't have to walk this messy road alone.

https://www.facebook.com/groups/bravemakers/

Coaching Packages

It's magic making time.

https://ktdean.com.au/work-together/

Get on the List

Join our girl gang to stay in the loop to receive free teachings, gifts, the latest and greatest news and upcoming events.

http://eepurl.com/Fwitz

Podcast: Simply Complicated

A podcast about bringing your human and not your halo. Life is beautifully messy and confusing then wonderful and challenging, so let's talk about it!

Simply Complicated with Katie Dean

Stay in touch

- **Website:** www.ktdean.com.au
- **Facebook:** www.facebook.com/ktdean.com.au
- **Instagram:** @ktdean.com.au

Messy Contributors

Ofa Fitzgibbons

Women's empowerment and embodiment coach and absolute legend.

www.goodfoodforthought.co

Insta @ofafitzgibbons

Renée Wilkinson

Newcastle based business owner, meditation guide, kinesiologist, yoga instructor, intuitive, and is such a powerful force for good in this world.

www.reneewilkinson.org

Insta @renee_wilkinson

Christal Fuentes

Relationship coach, author, and one hell of a siren.

www.theladiescoach.com

Insta @theladiescoach

Katherine Mackenzie Smith

Business and leadership coach, writer, and speaker championing introverted and highly sensitive leaders to find their own way to shine.

www.katherinemackenziesmith.com

Insta @miss_kms

Renee Mantle What can't she do? Events manager, marketing and communications rock star, Mumma, founder of Purposehood, and she is one of my best friends.

www.purposehood.com.au

Insta @purposehood

Acknowledgements

There is an entire village that comes together to create a book. Sure, the author writes the words but without a team to support, hold and steer her they are destined to become words written and forgotten.

Not here though. These words were loved, cared for and championed by a team who believed in the vision as much as I did.

> Natasha Gilmour – My editor. The captain of this ship and the woman who I don't think I could do this without. Thank you, for making this process what it is. I trust you and appreciate your unwavering guidance more than you'll ever know.

> Amy Molloy – You're a guiding light, your authenticity and encouragement with the framework for *Messy*, helped get us here. Thank you.

Amy – Secret Book Stuff – Thank you for seeing in me and encouraging my love for writing for writings sake. When the words weren't coming, thank you for reminding me that it's ok to love this part.

Niki Hennessey – My wing woman. My go-to gal. Just thank you. Thank you for being you and listening as I prattled on about ideas for this heart project.

Amy Mackenzie – Thank you for encouraging me to dream bigger and for helping me to see in me something I didn't know was there. You did though. Thank you for not letting me stay 'safe'. I adore you.

Glossary of Anti-Self-Help-y terminology

AFGO: another forking growth opportunity. Usually comes in the form of a really hectic life situation.

AF—: as fuck. To be fully immersed in the experience or description.

Back yourself: to truly support and believe in yourself. Ultimate goals.

Bejeezels: a phrase used to describe a moment of surprise. To scare the bejeezels out of you means that you were really, really scared.

Cluster-fucky: disastrous and incredibly poorly handled life event or situation.

Crapola: definitely not ideal. Quite crap really, but fancier.

Dang: usually used to describe an inopportune moment. Can be supplemented by damn, or darn.

Douche: a complete moron and someone we would like to avoid in general or avoid resembling.

Effing: more politically correct then dropping the F— Bomb. The F—bomb means fuck.

Emotion-o-metre: the ranges at which we feel things. The full emotional spectrum.

Enough-ness: that's what you are.

FFS: for fuck's sake, aka a phrase that's thrown around when everything goes to shit, and you're really frustrated. Like when you just sit down, and someone asks you to get up.

Forking: it's a way more polite way to say fucking. We're classy like that around here.

Fucktards: a really, really dense person.

Fudge it: a phrase that one might utter before they do something great. Especially if they way to say fuck, but they can't because little people are around.

Gig: an event of some kind. It just sounds cooler.

Human-ing: what we are doing right here, right now—our existence.

Internal compass: your intuition. Your GPS. Your guide for all things.

Life-force vampires: people who suck the life out of you who usually have no respect for your boundaries and are only interested in taking from you. To be avoided at all costs.

Life gig: this wild ride we call life. Our journey, our path and the messiness that being a person entails.

Meditation: necessary. It's a pause and reboot for your mind.

Probs: just easier to abbreviate than type probably, you get it!

Pwfffooooor: an over expression of wonderment.

Raise your vibe: to actively create more positive thoughts and a life that is more aligned with your ultimate self.

Radsters: generally, awesome people.

Rad life day: a day where everything flows, and it's filled with epic moments.

Shit tonne: a legit measurable term, also known as heaps.

Shizzle: a more gangsta way of saying 'shit'. Plus, it's fun to say.

Stoked: thrilled; delighted.

Superpower: the special qualities that we all have.

Tapped out: empty. Exhausted. Depleted.

Ultra-feely: super emotional and sensitive at a particular time.

WTF: what the fuck, I mean, seriously?

Yikes: a juvenile way of expressing alarm or concern.

www.ingramcontent.com/pod-product-compliance
Lightning Source LLC
Chambersburg PA
CBHW071857290426
44110CB00013B/1183